STRANGE JOURNEY

D0861991

STRANGE JOURNEY

HOW TWO HOMESICK PILGRIMS STUMBLED BACK INTO THE CATHOLIC CHURCH

*from the creators of the **Sick Pilgrim** blog*

**JESSICA MESMAN GRIFFITH
& JONATHAN RYAN**

LOYOLAPRESS.
A JESUIT MINISTRY
Chicago

LOYOLA PRESS.
A JESUIT MINISTRY

3441 N. Ashland Avenue
Chicago, Illinois 60657
(800) 621-1008
www.loyolapress.com

© 2017 Jessica Mesman Griffith & Jonathan Ryan
All rights reserved.

Scripture quotations contained herein are from the *New Revised Standard Version Bible: Catholic Edition*, copyright © 1993 and 1989 by the Division of Christian Education of the National Council of the Churches of Christ in the U.S.A. Used by permission. All rights reserved.

Cover and interior art credit: Rively/iStock/Thinkstock.

ISBN: 978-0-8294-4499-5
Library of Congress Control Number: 2017951834

Printed in the United States of America.
17 18 19 20 21 22 23 24 25 26 27 Tshore 10 9 8 7 6 5 4 3 2 1

CONTENTS

INTRODUCTION

Jessica Mesman Griffith

"Every branch of human knowledge, if traced up to its source and final principles, vanishes into mystery," wrote the weird paranormal fiction author Arthur Machen. I sent this quote to Jonathan after, at his urging, I finally read Machen's collected stories. Jonathan wrote back: "That pretty much sums up the entire story of our journeys to becoming Catholic again."

We were both born into the Church but spent much of our lives exploring dark alleys and strange paths in other realms—other churches, philosophies, and fascinations—that either dead-ended at despair or led us back to where we started. Science. Politics. Art. The occult. Hedonism. Gnosticism. Presbyterianism. They each frustrated us in turn. What might at first be thrilling ended up, as Walker Percy summed it up in *Lost in the Cosmos*, as merely "disappointing." When we did stumble into something that felt true and good, we'd begin to find it suspiciously familiar, like a tune we'd heard before, hummed in the cradle and lodged in the memory.

Oh, we'd realize. This is so . . . Catholic.

Jonathan was an editor at a publishing house (and now works in a parish) in addition to writing paranormal thrillers, and we met when he was canvassing for writers. He contacted me after reading some of my work in an old anthology. We met at an Irish-themed pub in South Bend to talk about the possibility of working together on a project. I was supposed to be pitching him a book.

The problem was, I was in the grip of a major depressive episode, and I wasn't much in the mood to write a book. Especially not a Catholic book. I didn't know how I felt about my religion anymore, or if I had a place in the church at all.

So, over our first beer, instead of pitching him a book, I told him about how when I was a teenager I used to try to contact my mother, who died of cancer when I was fourteen, through Ouija boards and call-in psychics and past-life readings and even mirror divination, and that I thought all this had led me back to the Catholic Church: I was looking for the dead.

When he laughed and said he'd also come back for the ghosts—and the exorcisms—I knew we'd be friends even if he didn't publish my book. I didn't know this at the time, but

Jonathan was just on the other side of a painful divorce and had come back to the Catholic Church after a fraught ending to his years as a Presbyterian pastor.

Maybe we sensed each other's grief or the earnestness of our bottomed-out need for something more than the world seemed to offer. Whatever it was, Jonathan knew I wasn't kidding or trying to shock him when I said dabbling in the occult had made me Catholic. It felt so good to confess to a fellow traveler that I'd tried just about everything under the sun to make contact with the unseen—and that none of it had worked.

Jonathan didn't condemn me. He wasn't shocked or appalled. And, most important, he didn't try to evangelize me out of my story. He believed me when I said I don't do those things anymore—though I'm often tempted—because I go to church. And he didn't judge me when I said I resist them, not because the Catholic Church says it's bad (I still do plenty of things my church says are bad; the church is much wiser than I), but because they are dead ends, and because I've found a better way. That when I read that St. Thérèse of Lisieux said her dead mother came to her—along with Jesus and all the saints—each time she received the Eucharist, I knew I'd be Catholic for life.

Hell yeah, he said.

Or something like that.

And that's how the blog, *Sick Pilgrim*, was born. Because we knew there had to be others. People like us, whose unconventional paths, losses, heartbreaks, and yearning for contact with divine mystery had led them to the doors of the church but left them there lonely, confused, and unsure of how to proceed.

Jonathan and I were born into Catholicism; in some ways, our returns were homecomings, and we felt united by a determination to reclaim what was rightfully ours, however undeserving we may be. But what about those who didn't have the courage or the sheer brattiness or even the naïveté to waltz in and claim a place at the table? Those who'd been turned off by an overly politicized faith? Those who can't agree with church teaching but still find their hearts and souls and imaginations to be thoroughly, irreversibly Catholic? What about the other wounded travelers who didn't realize they weren't walking alone?

That's why we decided to launch our blog. We asked our friend, artist Kate Plows, to design us a logo based on the stick figure my young daughter and I had been drawing for years, since she'd become obsessed with the seasick travelers on the *Mayflower*. I'd grown to see him as my personal mascot, this little traveler with his misshapen hat and *x*'s for eyes—bound for God in the end, however lost and battered he becomes on his journey.

At first, we thought the blog would be our virtual soapbox, and we took turns stepping up and talking to each other, hoping a few curious bystanders might show up to watch. But it quickly became more of a pub. Others started taking their turn at the mic. We told our stories: the true stories, the hard stories, the ones that you feel you probably shouldn't share in church, at least not outside the confessional. We confessed our love for a faith we sometimes found embarrassing. We excavated our unabashedly weird Catholic imaginations—formed by an ancient, mystical faith that seems out of step with our secular world—for mystery and magic. And, as more and more pilgrims began to stumble in, we started propping up one another, linking arms, and walking together.

This book, we hope, will take you on a journey too, as you walk with us through a year in the church—and through many years of our own journeys. We're going to tell you the stories of how we've found ourselves despite our tendencies to wander, of how we have been drawn ever deeper into the church, in pursuit of the mystery of faith.

ADVENT

THE NATIVITY OF BIGFOOT

Jonathan

My search for the mystery of faith started with a green light in the sky.

As a kid, I lived in Haubstadt, Indiana, a small town of 1,500 people that lost its entire downtown to a train wreck not long after my family moved to St. Louis. Residing in a village this small meant that you had to drive twenty minutes to get anywhere significant. And, when your family caught the fire of the Charismatic movement that burned its way through the Catholic Church in the late 1970s, that meant a weekly drive to Evansville, the nearest "big" town.

We took that long drive because our small parish didn't go in for that sort of spirit-filled, jumping-around-with-your-hands-raised nonsense. A diminutive pre-Vatican II monsignor ran our church with an iron fist and would often lapse back into Latin for short periods during the Mass.

On a particular Sunday, one of my friends served as an altar boy. He barely bumped the kneeler and jangled the *sanctus* bells reserved for the elevation of the host. The priest looked down at the server, his face contorted in anger. For weeks after that, none of us wanted to serve at Mass with the monsignor who had fiery eyes and the look of God's own death angel, straight from the book of Exodus.

But my parents paid no mind to his priestly anger. Instead, they packed my sister and me in the car to chase down the latest prayer meeting or healing service. On one of these drives, I played with my Transformer robot—"more than meets the eye." As I danced him across the back of my dad's seat, I noticed a strange green light in the sky. I watched as it flashed, blinked, and then stretched until it disappeared.

Gaping, I leaned forward in the seat and said, "Dad, Dad, I think I just saw a UFO!"

"A what?" He looked at me through the rearview mirror.

"You know, a UFO, a spaceship, like from Close Encounters of the Third Kind. Maybe it's from another planet."

He cleared his throat. "Son, I don't think it's a UFO."

"Oh. Why not?" I asked, sitting back in my seat.

"It doesn't matter. I want you to focus on tonight. You need to concentrate on the Lord. You need to start talking about the things of God. You're old enough."

I squirmed and tried not to interrupt my dad while he spoke. My little sister munched on her M&Ms. (I'm pretty sure she was born with a bag of them in her hands. The kid never went anywhere without them.)

"But, what if it was? Wouldn't it be cool?"

My dad raised his eyebrows, not a good sign. "Well, if it wasn't an airplane or helicopter, it's probably from the devil."

Scratching my head, I said, "Why? How do you know?"

He didn't say anything for a moment. Today, as a father myself, I realize what had left him speechless: He didn't have a real answer to give, so he fell back on a time-honored dad tradition and made one up.

"Well, because, Satan probably wants to distract you from the things of God. You need to pray about it."

I opened my mouth to argue, a permanent facial expression for me. But my dad kept his brows raised and then cocked his head to the side, a sure sign that I'd better shut up. He'd brought up "the things of God," and that meant serious business. He wasn't in the mood for a nuanced argument over theology and aliens.

Sighing, I looked out the window. I never understood why we drove all the way to Evansville for these prayer meetings. I liked our parish church, despite our wrathful priest. I liked eating Jesus and learning about the saints. When I went to

Mass, the chanted prayers, the singsong voice of the priest, and—on holy days—the smell of incense all fascinated and even scared me a little. When I walked into our parish church, I knew I'd entered the presence of something different. Something unlike anything else in my life.

Take, for example, the stories of the saints. There's nothing more glorious and frightening at the age of seven than to hear stories of the blessed of God. Padre Pio punctured by the stigmata: the nail wounds of Christ on the cross. St. Sebastian shot full of arrows. St. Lucy holding out her gouged eyes on a platter. Or, my personal hero and eventual name saint, St. Peter, hung upside down on a cross because he felt unworthy to die as Christ had.

Imagine these gruesome tales told by habited nuns as they waved their arms, black sleeves billowing and flowing with each dramatic gesture. The scary stories told around the campfire at Scout camp seemed boring by comparison.

But the charismatic prayer meetings scared me in a different, deeper way, one I didn't understand as a kid. When we first started attending, my sister and I went to childcare. While we played with the Tonka trucks, mini-basketballs, or Barbie dolls, we'd hear people shouting, screaming in tongues, and the preacher's yelling penetrating the paper-thin walls. None of us could make out what was going on, but we tried not think about it. We had our cookies and juice, pretending not to notice the strange noises while talking about anything but God.

One day, my dad came to me and said, "I think you're old enough to come to the meetings, at least for part of them."

Curious to find out about all the screaming and yelling, I agreed. I wanted to know what made the preacher so angry and why everyone cried. The fateful night arrived, and I sat on the gray metal folding chair. Everyone filed in with wide smiles, hugging one another tight. I sat up straight when I saw a flock of nuns and a few priests enter. What, I wondered, were they doing here? Didn't they know this wasn't Mass?

The music started, and I had to admit, it beat the out-of-tune organ of St. Peter and Paul Parish. Sure, the lead singers couldn't really carry a tune. But they had drums, and I loved drums. I tapped my foot along with the beat and clapped my hands as people started grooving to Jesus rock.

After the forty-five-minute Holy Spirit jam session, I wanted to be back playing with trucks and eating cookies. A man with slicked-back hair, skinny as a rail and wearing a gray suit with a tie so wide only the 1970s would understand, had started preaching.

He couldn't stop talking about the devil. The devil had control over our country. The devil was in the pants of every teenager. The devil. The devil. The devil. The preacher talked as if he and the devil had been old friends and then had a terrible falling out.

He lathered himself up into a sweat as he yelled, "And we've got this rock and roll. It's about *sexxxx!*"

Sex? What's that about? I'd heard it mentioned only vaguely by friends at school in whispers so the sisters wouldn't hear.

"Yesss, my brothers and sisters. The devil is using this rock music to lead teenagers into sex with African-inspired Voodoo beats. They grind their hips against each other. It's like Mike Warnke said, there is a whole underground network of devil worshippers looking to claim our children, and they murder babies in secret rituals after having orgies."

I shifted in my seat. Never mind that they'd just played rock music with drums during worship. If Mike Warnke said it, it must be true. He was my favorite Christian comedian, and supposedly he had been a satanic high priest. Along with his hilarious comedy sets, he told spine-tingling tales of cutting his arm for blood rituals and all the drugs he took during satanic orgies. Heady stuff for a seven-year-old kid. Later, in 1991, the Protestant magazine *Cornerstone* ran a damning exposé of his whole story, revealing it to be an utter fraud.

Oddly, Warnke had grown up Catholic but left the church. He chose lying to people about his entire life instead.

I didn't know about that then. All I knew was that I didn't want to be with the devil. I didn't like him. The preacher screamed that we must have Jesus in our hearts or we would be slaves to the satanic majesty. The whole thing unsettled me, and I thought about it the entire drive home. No, I didn't want to be the devil's. I must belong to Jesus.

I piped up, "Dad, I want to ask Jesus into my heart when I get home. Can I?"

My dad looked up and beamed. "That's great, son. I'm so proud of you! We will pray right when we get home!"

Sitting in the enclosed stairway of our old farmhouse, my dad prayed with me and then hugged me, whispering into my ear, "I'm so proud of you, son. So proud."

I loved that my dad was proud of me, but everything else confused me. Wasn't Jesus already inside me, every time I ate his body during daily Mass at my Catholic school? And why did I fear the devil more than I loved Jesus? I felt divided, unsure, stuck between these two worlds of Catholicism—the Mass and the charismatic meetings.

I was hearing two theologies. When I went to St. Peter and Paul school, they told me to eat the Eucharist, confess my sins, and do good to others, and then Jesus would be happy. It seemed wonderful and strange. But the charismatic preachers screamed about the devil; the only way to ward him off was to be "righteous" and ask Jesus into your heart. Both theologies seemed full of mystery and strangeness, but only the former brought me any comfort. The confusion shattered my faith into pieces. I've spent most of my life trying to put them back together.

Enter the green light.

As we continued driving to the prayer meeting after I saw the UFO, I pretended to examine my soul dutifully as my dad wanted. But all I could think about was aliens and life on other planets. This was a tangible mystery, something I could really think about and ponder at the age of seven, the mystery of God lost in the jumble of Charismatic Hallelujahs and black-habited nuns. God had gotten too confusing to me. I wondered if there were any other strange mysteries out there. I'd never ask my parents, but I knew if I waited for a trip to my Grandma's, I find the answers with her library card.

Every summer, I went to her house for two weeks. She and my grandfather owned a baseball-card store in Hutingburg, Indiana, and I spent many days helping them there. I loved baseball and collecting the cards. When I was at my own house, I would often dig through the cushions of the couch to find loose change so that I could go to the little drugstore across the street to buy baseball cards.

Even better than all the baseball cards, my grandma gave me her library card, a great thing for a kid with an urge to search out the mysterious, the uncanny, and the paranormal. I didn't use it to check out anything so obvious as Stephen King books, though. My cousins loved his books and would talk about them all the time, but the preachers had screamed that reading Stephen King would open the door to the devil. If my grandma told my parents that I was reading *IT*, they probably would have had me exorcised. Instead, I chose the subtler route, checking out books on UFOs, Bigfoot, ghost stories, and finally, my own personal bogeyman, the Mothman of western Virginia.

Grandma never checked on my books, and if she saw a collection of ghost stories, she didn't seem to care. After all, as a Catholic, she embraced the idea that the dead are always with us. She'd talk to St. Anthony every time she lost her car keys or pray to the Blessed Mother for my grandpa to get home safely from a long trip in his truck.

After she went to bed, I'd lie awake, window open, and listen to the train thunder past about three hundred feet from the house. I would read into the early morning, my skin prickling every time I read about Bigfoot walking in front of someone's car on a dark road, or the ghost of a dead relative appearing to a loved one to say good-bye.

Was this just an elementary school rebellion against my parents? Was it me trying to be my own person? If you'd asked me then, I probably would have said, "Because I like getting goose bumps."

I didn't read about the paranormal to escape from the world. My parents were not abusive monsters. But my confusion about God and our two very different church lives had led me away from God and God's mysteries. But we are built for mystery. It's a part of who we are as humans. It's what we want out of life, a quest for the unknown.

My parents helped keep the search for mystery in my heart, even if they didn't know it. They didn't allow me, of course, to watch horror films such as *Nightmare on Elm Street*. Their rules about horror movies pushed me further into the stranger parts of my heart and brain. By letting Bigfoot, ghosts, and the Mothman (*shudder*) into my life, I discovered a deeper sense of the possible weirdness of the world. Things were not always as they seemed. The unseen world might break through into our world at any moment. It seemed just as likely as crossing the street on any given day. But if the unseen broke into the seen, I didn't know what would happen. Maybe something awesome. Maybe something terrible. Anything was possible.

Still, I couldn't understand how Jesus or the church fit into that kind of unseen mysteries. They seemed like separate worlds to me. I still believed in Christ with all my heart. But our parish priest didn't seem to be on very good terms with my dad. Everyone in our conservative German Catholic town was convinced we were wackos. We got phone calls at night, devils drawn on our windows. I got into a fight at school when people called my mom and dad terrible names.

But that didn't stop my investigation into weirdness. Fortunately for me, my mom's aunt lived in Vincennes, Indiana, ground zero for all kinds of strange tales. People talk of a purple-headed monster that haunts a local bridge. There have been numerous sightings of UFOs over the years. My cousins insisted their house was haunted. Wanting to investigate, I asked them one day to "prove it."

Their response was to take me into their basement. In the back wall, a gaping, dark hole dared us to explore. Part of me knew it was just the unfinished part of the basement, but I couldn't be sure.

"What's in there?" I asked.

"We think it's a portal," my cousin Aaron said.

"What's that?"

"You know, where the spirits come in and out, like a doorway."

We all stood there, waiting for the first person to go inside.

"Have you ever been inside?" I asked, trembling a little.

They looked at me as if I'd lost my mind. At that moment, something clinked and clunked in the dark hole in the wall. We ran outside, hearts racing, adrenaline pumping, all of us wanting it to happen again, always seeking the thrill of the unknown.

Later that night, my cousin Wendy sat us down to tell us a real story about the Knox County monster. In the late 1970s, Bigfoot mania gripped the nation. Several sightings were reported in southern Indiana, some right near Vincennes.

With the adults out for the evening, Wendy was in charge. We sat on the floor at her feet as she said, "One night, a couple heard their dog barking, but they didn't think anything of it. Stupid animal often barked at its own shadow, they thought."

She lowered her eyes and then looked up. "Yes, that's what they thought, but they were wrong."

Hunching forward, my cousins and I gripped our pillows to our chests.

"The next morning, they went outside to check on the dog, a huge German shepherd. He was whimpering and shaking and wouldn't come out of his doghouse. When the couple walked back to their house, they notice huge pieces of siding stripped off and deep claw marks grooved into the house. Some kind of dark fur and blood stuck to the wood. And there were large footprints in the yard."

I hugged myself to stop from shivering. Later I couldn't sleep. The adults came back, and I plied them with questions. They confirmed that everything happened the way my cousin had described. I wanted to drive by the house and go into the woods. Would they take me there?

They all laughed at me and told me to go to bed. That night, as I lay listening to the unexplained noises in the house, I didn't understand why the adults laughed off the whole Knox County monster. Had Bigfoot shown up? If he had, wouldn't that mean something? Wouldn't that give me answers to the nagging ache, the sense of mystery, the desire to know something that has always been unknowable? Why wasn't this vitally important to the adults in my life? I didn't understand them or why they didn't take it seriously. Didn't they wonder too, about a potential mystery in their midst, waiting to be born out of the darkness of the Midwest?

HE SHALL BE A LIGHT

Jessica

Every year, on the first Sunday of Advent, my dad would disappear into the dark portal of our attic while I waited at the foot of the ladder. I wasn't allowed to step even on the first rung—this was a dangerous undertaking—but I could help by holding the ladder steady as it creaked under his weight. One by one, he'd pass the hollow plastic figures down into my hands, and I'd wipe the dust from their crowns with an old beach towel. We had the full set, though they were melted in spots from being stored in an attic in the Louisiana heat: Mary, Joseph, the Three Wise Men, two sleeping sheep, a donkey with a saddle, baby Jesus in a manger. We arranged them reverently in the front yard and lit them up by a long orange extension cord.

When we flipped the switch at twilight, I waited for my dad to go inside so he wouldn't tease me, and then I'd kneel in the damp grass next to the Wise Men and say a Hail Mary and an Our Father. We were Catholic and went to Mass every Sunday, and I went to Catholic school, but our family didn't pray together. It was a private matter reserved for bedtime, when I was alone in the darkness. Still, it seemed right to me, as a child, to mark the climactic moment of illumination with prayer.

I could see the glowing nativity from my bedroom window. For a few days, I'd resist the urge to go out and cradle the baby Jesus in my arms and wrap him in a cloth to complement his plastic diaper. I also worried that doing so might be sacrilegious. But inevitably I'd give in to the temptation. Waiting to be sure nobody was looking, I'd lift him from the manger. Year after year, I enacted this private drama, always surprised by his lightness. The other figures were filled with sand so they wouldn't topple in the wind or blow down the street in a storm as our garbage cans did—still plenty of thunder and rain in a Louisiana winter. But the infant was light as a feather.

Now that I have my own home and children, I have disregarded the norms of tasteful bourgeois Christmas decorations—monochromatic or topiary trees, real pine boughs, an amaryllis or two in sleek, modern pots—and purchased my own light-up nativity set for the front yard, remembering my powerful attraction to that glowing Holy Family in residence just outside my bedroom window all through Advent,

Christmas, and sometimes, depending on my dad's schedule, well into February.

Our neighbors were also Catholic—most people in southeastern Louisiana are—but they weren't the type to have a light-up nativity in the front yard. Instead, they had a more tasteful crèche in their bay window. From our driveway, I could just see the three elegant white figures: Mary and Joseph bowing over the baby, swaddled in real white cloth and resting stiffly in a wooden manger, all of them bathed in soft blue light. I imagined they were carved from alabaster, a word I had to look up in the dictionary because it was in a song I loved at the time, "Wrapped around Your Finger," by the Police. I thought everything our neighbors did was fancy. But it turns out that their figurines were plastic too.

Sometimes, after borrowing an egg or delivering a message from my mother, I'd stand before our neighbors' bay window, gazing past my reflection at the scene. I can still imagine myself there, in my memory, conjuring my disheveled pigtails and wrinkled uniform blouse. Once a reporter from the *Slidell Sentry News* took my picture in that place for the "Neighbors" section of the Sunday paper.

Years later, when I visited at Christmas, I saw that newspaper clipping framed and hanging in their house among their family photos, and I suddenly remembered being caught there at my little ritual, feeling simultaneously embarrassed and honored.

I was a child who loved rituals. I had a very orderly prayer life but also had to tap things in my room and in the car a certain number of times and in the right order or I'd feel the world spinning off its axis. Back then, we didn't know, or didn't talk about, things such as obsessive-compulsive disorder or Asperger's syndrome. And I probably kept most of this stuff to myself anyway. But my parents didn't mark me as particularly unusual. I had strange habits and fears and spent a lot of time alone, but I was a straight-A student. No cause for concern. Yet.

Every year on December 23, the neighbors with the "alabaster" crèche threw a little Christmas Eve party at which all the neighborhood children received some small gift. It was an event we all looked forward to, what seemed like hundreds of people crushed into the warmth of their modest ranch-style home, which was filled with the glow of candles and Christmas lights and the sounds of classic carols on the turntable. Their home always felt like a little church to me, filled with icons and statuary and leather-bound books with colorful ribbons, whereas the only books in our house were the paperbacks I bought at the Bookshelf on Fremaux Avenue with my report-card money—*Babysitters Club*, *Sweet Valley High*, and later, works by V. C. Andrews and Anne Rice.

By the time I turned thirteen, the sacred atmosphere of that house was an enormous comfort to me. It was my constant, the only thing in my life that hadn't changed. My mother was sick. My parents had left our traditional parish with the somber and magnificent Monsignor Hotard at the helm for an Evangelical Protestant world of Osteen family-like ministers and their ilk: those who promised faith healings to true believers. I'd gone with them, of course, submitting my last shred of thirteen-year-old dignity to be baptized, full-immersion style, in a Jacuzzi bathtub—never mind that Father Hotard had baptized me as an infant. I had to do it all again, and this time, with feeling. That is, if I wanted my mother to live. And of course I wanted, more than anything, for my mother to live. I would have given anything for the miracle we needed to reverse stage IV metastatic lung cancer. Giving up Catholicism seemed a small price to pay, although it also meant giving up school and friends and secular music and movies and entering a new world of Trick or Trunk and Carmen concerts. I remember how grateful and proud my mother looked when I told her I'd gone up for the altar call and accepted Jesus as my personal Lord and Savior.

But I never could believe that the church of my childhood was the whore of Babylon, as the new preacher proclaimed. I slept with my rosary under my pillow. I read my vampire books under the covers. And later, after my mother died, I worried that maybe I'd sabotaged any chance we'd had at witnessing a miracle.

That year, on Little Christmas Eve (the traditional name for December 23) I walked across the wet grass to the neighbors' house in my black tights, black dress, and way too much black eyeliner. I was listening to Depeche Mode on my headphones, and I'd outgrown sitting on Santa's lap, so instead, I wove my way through the crowd, sneaked some rum into my Coke, and retreated to their backyard, alone, to lie in the hammock and watch the stars.

In the darkness I could just make out the dark lines of their shed, where on a night years before, their golden spaniel, named Mandy, for the Barry Manilow song, had given birth to a litter. The neighbors' daughter led us into the dimness that night, and we crouched at a safe distance while the puppies emerged as tiny brown sacks. I was little enough that when one of them died, I was shocked by its fragility. At thirteen, though, I dwelled instead on the improbability that anything so small and fragile should live.

My own mother was in bed back at our house, suffering her latest toxic dose of chemo, dying at age thirty-five.

As I lay there in the hammock, I began to feel a little drunk and sentimental. Also cold. Winter in Louisiana is damp and chilly. When I went back inside, the house was filled with chatter and the clinks of glasses, its rooms warm and woody and dark but for the glow from the tree and the spotlight on the crèche in the window.

"A present for Jessie!" Santa bellowed, handing me a small package wrapped in silver paper.

Embarrassed but secretly pleased, I shouldered through the local dignitaries, out the front door, back across the grass to our house, quiet and dark so my mother could rest. I went to my room and shut the door, pressed play on New Order, "Everything's Gone Green," a song with lyrics about the confusion sprung up from devotion. "Show me, please show me the way," the singer pleads, to an incongruently frenetic dance beat. I opened my gift, a book, *Writing Down the Bones*, by Natalie Goldberg, a classic guidebook for engaging in the writing life. I prized it above all other presents that year. Mostly because I felt that someone had finally taken me seriously. I read it cover to cover, again and again, lingered over the inscription on the inside of the cover. It was a vote of confidence in my promise as a writer, all I'd ever wanted to be.

Still, I could never think of anything to write. I'd sit, pen in hand, mood music in the background, and end up doodling the initials of the boy I loved. I wasn't ready to be a writer. Not then.

I hadn't realized that my mind's obsession with pattern making, with congruity, could manifest as wonder, as worship, and as an impulse toward creation. I was oblivious to the way Mandy's puppies, sleeping quietly in my mind in the glowing blue light of the crèche, had merged with the blazingly tacky Holy Family in the yard outside my window, my own mother suffering in her bed in the next room. But I was beginning to sense those connections, the bright lines that mark the path from A to B.

I didn't yet have the words, only the inclination, the gentle nudge to observe, to kneel, to pray.

CHRISTMAS

I'M NOT AFRAID OF THE DARK

Jonathan

"Are you afraid of the dark, Daddy?"

My seven-year-old stared up at me with her Cindy Lou Who blue eyes, hoping for some kind of comfort that would help her sleep. I tucked her hair behind her ears and said something she probably didn't expect from her dad.

"I am. But I love it too."

Most of us avoid taking any sort of journey in the dark unless we have some kind of light. And when it comes to the journey of trying to figure out God, the darkness is the last thing we want. We've been taught to fear it, avoid it, or deny it, but never to embrace it. My daughter certainly didn't understand my answer as she wrinkled her nose at me and asked me to turn on her night-light. For me, though, my path to the Catholic Church has always been shrouded in darkness guided by one little point of light.

In the ancient Hebrew temple, a massive curtain veiled the Holy of Holies. No one was allowed to go in except for the chief priest, and he entered only once a year. No candles lit the darkness, and only the Ark of the Covenant, when it was still around, occupied the sacred space. Contrary to myth, the priest never wore a rope with a bell, in case God decided to strike him dead because he was unclean. In fact, the priest entered the dark on Yom Kippur to offer atonement for the sins of the people. And there, he met God, performed his priestly duty, and the sins of the people were forgiven. All this in the dark—with no candles, no outside light, no nothing. I often tried to imagine myself in the place of that priest. What did he feel? Terror? Elation? Love? I'm guessing all the above.

The idea of the darkness in the Holy of Holies dominated Jewish and Christian contemplatives. King David sings about finding God in the quietness of the night and the struggle when everything turns dark. People in the Middle Ages called it finding God in the "cloud of unknowing."

And yet many people think of Christianity as responsible for hatred of the dark, for equating darkness with evil. Recently, I read *The End of Night*, by Paul Bogard, about how light pollution is slowly killing us by interrupting our sleep patterns and natural rhythms. He makes his argument well, but he completely misunderstands the Judeo-Christian view of darkness. While he doesn't directly blame artificial light pollution on Christianity, he implies it, as if the darkening of the great dance of heaven, as C. S. Lewis called it, is somehow our fault.

The truth is, Christians never believed that the dark itself was evil. Rather, darkness is a time when we can't see very clearly and need the light of God to guide us. Which, if we are honest, could be said of nearly every moment in our lives. There are times when I wake up in the morning and everything seems dark. I feel lost.

When we do get lost—and we do—it's often hard to tell what's God and what's not. But contemplative mystics such as St. John of the Cross believed that God could be met in the darkness in a way he cannot be met in the blazing light of day. During the times of the light, we trust ourselves and our senses, not realizing the reason we see at all is because of the light God gives. He removes that light not as a punishment but as way to encourage us to reach out and grab his hand.

I learned to love and fear the darkness in the Midwest, a place that drips with an atmospheric heaviness that's often difficult to describe to people from sunnier climes. The gray sky takes over around November and lasts until April. There are times when I feel as if I live in permanent twilight.

My friends who live in exotic places such as Utah or Oregon believe I live in a Wendell Berry novel or an episode of *A Prairie Home Companion*. Homey and warm, if a little backward. Certainly not a place to encounter the mystery of God or the vibrating presence of the unseen world.

It's true that on our concrete highways we often race by landscapes, oblivious to the hints and whispers that point us to the unseen just waiting to be noticed. It takes effort, time, and a saint-like patience to slow down and behold, as Elisha's servant did in 2 Kings, the reality around us. People in America seem especially prone to wearing their provincial blinders. We're convinced that we have to go an exotic location like Machu Picchu or jump the pond to the haunted green hills of Ireland.

I used to be apologetic about where I grew up. I bashed it more than anyone else. "I hate it here," I would say emphatically. "There's nothing but boring cornfields." You could say I was a Luke Skywalker–grade whiner, always looking to where he was going and not to where he already was or what he was doing.

But, even during those times, the landscape worked its dark magic on me. It's true, the Midwest doesn't have the moss-covered trees of a Louisiana bayou or the dark, forbidding forests of the Appalachian Mountains. But the hidden places of the Midwest harbor a number of strange and unusual secrets, and they creep me out. The landscape, emptied decades ago at the height of the Rust Belt migration, feels haunted, and there are places where the veil between the seen and unseen worlds is like water. Old ghosts of frustrated lives, the absence of people who've moved on to other lands. Life has been hard in most of the Midwest since the factories closed or moved on to better tax breaks.

In such a lonely atmosphere, it's hard not to feel a tingle of the spine, a lurch in the stomach, and fear of the dark. This is especially true if you grew up in an old farmhouse at the edge of town, with an imagination nursed by the kinds of books I read as a kid. That farmhouse was haunted, without question. One night, my dad woke up to hear someone opening the door to the enclosed stairway that led upstairs. He tried to get up but couldn't.

An old farmer with hate in his eyes came into the room and stared at him. He shook his head at my dad and disappeared. To this day, my dad can't say for sure if it was a dream or something evil.

I suffered from terrible nightmares. Usually, they consisted of tall, thin beings with big dark eyes and wide, gaping, toothless mouths. In my dreams, they would move their mouths to speak, and their voices would echo in my head. I don't remember most of the things they said, but very often they threatened my family or predicted terrible things for my life.

In one dream, they were in the living room lurking in the dark while members of my family talked loudly in the lights-ablaze kitchen. I tried to get to them, but the beings wouldn't allow it. They held me down on the couch, and I struggled to get free. They threatened that if I told anyone about their existence when I went into the light, they would do terrible things. Much later, I learned that the legendary horror writer H. P. Lovecraft had similar dreams; he called the beings "the gaunts." Whatever they were, they made me wake up, sweating and full of fear.

So, how did I learn not to fear the dark?

When I discovered that God loves and inhabits the darkness, it was during Christmas Eve Mass. And I clung to that belief as a child, even as the rest of my faith life shattered into pieces. As good German Catholics, we always went to Mass the day before Christmas, even as the Charismatic renewal was drawing my parents away from the Catholic Church. Even though I attended Mass every day as a Catholic-school requirement, "Christ Mass" was special. The veil between the seen and the unseen was thinner, as if angels would break through any moment over the barren farm fields of Haubstadt and sing "Gloria in Excelsis Deo" to the people of the Midwest.

The mystery of Christmas started to descend when, still in our drafty farmhouse, we bundled ourselves up and set out into the gloaming to walk a half a mile to the church. The north wind blew in our faces and made our eyes water. We huddled close together, looking at the Christmas lights that burst out with gaudy colors in the darkness of the town. My sister crunching on M&Ms, my mom and dad chatting about a prayer meeting, and me, contemplating the mystery of God coming in a manager.

Just about every Catholic church in America has what they call the Children's Mass on Christmas Eve. Everyone gets to smile at kids stumbling over words like Caesar Augustus as their cowlicks bob in rhythm while they make their way to the altar with the gifts. I usually participated in some way, either doing the readings, bringing up the gifts, or even being a server. I can't remember exactly what I did. But what always gripped me was the warm darkness of the church. Our priest always turned out the hanging lights and relied on either the lectern lights or the candles. Say what you want about Catholics, but we know how to nail atmosphere.

You'd think because of my dreams, I'd be afraid of *this* dark. But with everyone around me, huddled together on the wooden pews, the darkness felt a little less intimidating. I looked around at my friends and neighbors as we thought about Christmas. Given how poor we were, I'm sure my parents were stressed, hoping that my sister and I would love our Christmas presents.

But, the stresses of life seemed to fall away during this holy night. When the priest came up the aisle, swinging the censor, filling the church with the musty holy scent of myrrh, we knew it was time to celebrate God coming down in the flesh, born in the shit and the straw in some obscure town in Palestine known as Bethlehem. As far as we know, our Lord was born in the dark, with probably very little candlelight to help baby Jesus into the world.

As the Mass progressed to its high point, the elevation of the host, we could feel the anticipation of God coming to us. The drama of the Mass pushing us toward Bethlehem, to the stable when the world contained the Word. All of us at Mass drew closer together and leaned forward as the priest spoke the words of consecration and the bread was transformed by divine power into the very body of Christ, filling up the small stone church with his holy presence.

I walked up, only eight years old, to take the Body and the Blood. The dark no longer held the power of fear in the light of what, to the naked eye, was a round piece of paper-like substance and wine bought from a nearby monastery—in reality the very Body and Blood of Christ. Yet when I felt the glowing warmth of the wine, I knew that no "gaunts," no bad dreams, and no evil would touch us on that night.

And then we would walk home, my poor dad drunk on communion wine. As one of the Eucharistic ministers, he helped the priest drink the leftover wine from communion. This usually didn't present much of a problem except for the high holy days of Christmas Eve and Easter, when there were multiple Masses to serve. And in a small town, it was often difficult to find people to serve on the holidays.

You can imagine what drinking leftover wine from four Masses could do to a person. My dad would walk home with us, stumbling a little, laughing, and my mom would chuckle, saying he was drunk on the spirit, a good Charismatic way to describe it.

My parents made us go to bed right when we got home, but I could never sleep. The joke in my family is that I was so excited for presents that I would shake in anticipation. This is only partially true. I usually shook with joy. I knew I no longer had to fear the dark because Jesus had met me there in the Eucharist.

I couldn't have told you that at age eight. I wouldn't have been able to put together the ache for mystery I encountered in my paranormal books and the mystery of the Eucharist. They seemed to be two separate things, and no one helped me see it any differently. That unresolved tension pulled at me until it tore my life apart.

I realize now that my life reflected something in our fragmented culture, the church included, that teaches us to compartmentalize and dissect our life to death. We want to take out the mystery of things, but we can't help searching for it. That unresolved tension can be seen in the movies and stories that people can't get enough of, from the *Lord of the Rings* to *The Conjuring* to *Stranger Things*. We relish the uncanny. We yearn for the drama of the searching for the unknown. We sense that there is something else going on, buried in the ordinary. We know it, even if we can't prove it, showing there is more than one way to discover truth.

Meanwhile, church, which should be ushering us into these mysteries, has become boring, sterile, secularized, almost feeling like a business meeting or a rock concert. We no longer feel that we've entered a sacred space when we enter a Catholic church, a space where something different is happening. Often there's no visible tabernacle, no sanctuary candle, no incense, no sacred music. We've started to chase the latest worship fads and curricula, to dumb down the Mass or focus on making bigger parking lots. All of this comes from a good impulse, to meet people where they are, but the problem is, I don't really think most of us *know* what we need anymore, what we truly long for. We've been trained to think we need entertainment and convenience. But this isn't why we go to church. No wonder numbers are dwindling.

People see Catholics at worship, mumbling rote prayers and chanting and standing and sitting and kneeling, and they assume we are bored or checked out or on autopilot—and surely some of us are. But not all. Some of us are relying on the time-tested powers of ritual and repetition to enter a new space—a space of story, quest, and mystery.

As a child, I discovered that the light really does shine in the darkness. But it would take me thirty years to really understand it.

THE HOLY INNOCENTS: A SUDDEN PATCH OF SUNLIGHT IN THE DARK

Jessica

After Christmas, Catholics celebrate the feasts of martyrs: on December 26, St. Stephen, who was stoned to death for his faith, and, even more disturbing, on December 28, the Holy Innocents—the infant boys of Bethlehem who were murdered at Herod's command as he sought to destroy the Christ child.

This is the kind of thing that gets us Catholics accused of being morbid. But morbidity has never scared me. I need for my religion to look death in the face. I love that the church acknowledges that life is sometimes (often?) terrible and that the innocent suffer. Sometimes it looks as if the good guys lost.

All this is true. And yet we dare to hope because we believe that we're living in the same story as those who have suffered and died, and that this story isn't over yet. We too have a role to play.

I think of the *Lord of the Rings* story of Aragorn at the Battle of Helm's Deep, looking to the dawn for hope as the Orcs taunt him with certain death. He's outnumbered, and the bad guys know it. Things really are just terrible sometimes. Being a Christian doesn't protect us from that terror, but it can change our posture. When faced with death, loss, humiliation, or certain failure, it is good and right to mourn what shouldn't be; we weren't made for this distress. But we can, at the same time, be like Aragorn, and look to the dawn.

Feeling the beauty of the coming dawn is how I feel on Christmas morning. Though Easter is the high point of the church year, Advent and Christmas are a new beginning, moments of hopeful promise, a glorious exhale when God finally breaks through, the caesura between the virgin birth and Herod's wrath, the looming shadow of the cross. God is with us. Whom shall we fear?

On Christmas mornings in my early childhood, our joy was so great that my dad and our neighbors used to meet in the front yard to try to turn the world around so we could do it all again. My mom filmed them once: my dad and Mr. Sam in their bathrobes with their tumblers of Bloody Marys, chanting and bowing in some made-up ritual meant to turn back time.

The church recognizes that desire, in a way. The liturgical calendar is cyclical, not linear, and we come around again and again to the birth of Christ. We don't retrace our steps so much as we spiral deeper and deeper into the story as we grow another year older. We progress on our journeys by going further up and further in, as C. S. Lewis wrote in *The Last Battle*.

When I think of my dad and Mr. Sam now, I remember the story in Ray Bradbury's *Dandelion Wine* about a family who collected the golden weeds of high summer and pressed their liquor into glass bottles to line their basement shelves, so that in the dead of winter they could tiptoe down and commune "with a last touch of a calendar long departed." The words *dandelion wine*, for the narrator, are repeated as a mantra; they uncork a "sudden patch of sunlight in the dark." We might say that Christmas does the same, for all of us. For a moment, we can bask in the light, even if it's just the light of the bulbs on the tree.

But only a moment. Herod is coming. And we each will face our Herod, somehow, some time.

The young Douglas, who comes of age in Bradbury's stories, suffers from the dawning awareness that to be alive is to watch good things pass away. The story of a perfect summer is marred by its inevitable ending, by the departure of his dear friend John Huff, by the thrilling but terrifying discovery of his body as a "clock gold-bright and guaranteed to run"—and thus to run out. This is a recurring theme in Bradbury's works, and the young Douglas who wakes up to his mortality isn't so far from the guy who is tormented by his own skeleton, a memento mori that supports his very being.

Of course, this isn't just Bradbury's theme. It's humanity's cry.

I've always turned to books in times of grief, for distraction and consolation. I'm not sure why I expect to find consolation there, because I'm almost always met with a collective protest against the running of the clock. I see this protest in Shakespeare's Sonnet 73:

> That time of year you mayst in me behold
> When yellow leaves, or none, or few, do hang
> Upon those boughs which shake against the cold,
> Bare ruined choirs, where late the sweet birds sang.

I find it in children's books too: Leo Lionni's tale of Frederick the mouse, who collects the words of summer as a stay against winter's bleak and hungry nights; J. M. Barrie's Mrs. Darling, who exclaims to the flower-bearing Wendy, "Oh, why can't you remain like this forever!"

But Bradbury's Douglas, like my dad and like Mr. Sam, tries his best to stop time from passing. Douglas decides in *Dandelion Wine* that the only way to keep things slow is to watch everything and do nothing. He shouts angrily at dear John Huff when he sees him, on his last day in town, running in play, because he thinks John is running out their last hours together.

First, Douglas tries to convince John that it's earlier than it is by winding his watch back, but John, the realist, can tell by the sun's fading that the day is ending. Then Douglas attempts to freeze him, literally, in a game of statues, and as he circles his motionless friend in the twilight, Bradbury circles his conjured memories on the page, uncorks the bottle and finds "John Huff with grass stains on his knees . . . cuts on his fingers . . . with the quiet tennis shoes . . . the mouth that chewed . . . the eyes, not blind like statues' eyes, but filled with molten green gold."

"'John, now,' commands Douglas, 'don't you move so much as an eyelash. I absolutely command you to stay here and not move at all for the next three hours!'

'I got to go,' he whispers."

I think of my dad and Mr. Sam, standing in the dewy grass on a Christmas morning in southern Louisiana, their hands stretched toward the sun, my mother alive and well.

Her laughter. My joy. Like Douglas, I wind my watch and play at statues. And, like Bradbury, I conjure the moment and step inside.

"Don't you move so much as an eyelash."

Gather, press, store.

I line pages with words, as Douglas lines shelves with glittering bottles.

I have written my own moment not just to preserve it but to reanimate it.

Dandelion Wine. Dandelion Wine.

Behind all the literary references to despair at time's passage, I see a longing for the perfection we sense is our destiny, and the destiny of all we love and find beautiful: an endless summer, a golden flower that doesn't fade, a child that doesn't grow old, a mother who doesn't get sick. We want time—always, we want more of it. But we want it unsullied by the pressure to remember the good things in their perfection—"oh, why can't you remain like this forever?!"—before they slip into shadow. We want goodness to endure.

It's like we know we are built for eternity, only something has gone terribly wrong.

Like Douglas and John Huff, Mrs. Darling, Frederick the Mouse, and even Shakespeare, I can't escape chronos, the brutal forward march of clock time. The perfect moment will end. (And, I say thankfully, so will the imperfect.) Christmas joy will run with the blood of martyrs. My mother will die in the fall of my freshman year of high school.

As much joy as there is on Christmas morning, there's nothing quite so painful as Christmas in mourning. All the beloved rituals and traditions feel empty at best. I don't remember anything specific about our first Christmas without my mother. Not even the sadness. There's a hole there, an empty pocket. I'm sure we ate next door at Mr. Sam's—our neighbors fed us nearly all our meals by then. But there was no laughter, no meeting in the yard to attempt to turn back time. None of us wanted that Christmas to last. If we even remembered that silly ritual, it was with a stab in the heart.

Dandelion Wine.

If only. If only.

But this is why, when I came back to the church as an adult, I appreciated the martyrs of Christmastide. I knew by then, and all too well, that even as we celebrate the coming of our salvation and cry out our joy to the world, that we will mourn for all we've lost, all we must yet lose.

And still, like Aragorn, we look east and wait for the dawn.

EPIPHANY: HOW THE MAGOS CAME BACK INTO MY LIFE

Jonathan

One of the strangest paths I took to the Catholic Church led through a beautiful conservative Presbyterian college perched on the top of Lookout Mountain in Georgia. You can see seven states on a clear morning from the overlook in front of the main building of the college, Carter Hall. The once-famous Castle in the Clouds, a 1920s luxury hotel, looks very much like the hotel in *The Shining*.

I arrived fully immersed in the Charismatic movement of my parents, fully buying into the need for tongues, signs, and wonders. Catholicism I had left in the dust, and I thought I'd found the mystery I craved. I considered myself a mystic and believed that I had a secret knowledge of the Holy Spirit these Presbyterians would never get.

But I soon discovered a world I never knew existed: smart, thinking, and well-read Christians. In my Charismatic circles,

I'd been told that I thought too much and that doing so would interfere with my relationship with God. I learned to keep my love for books hidden and my questioning nature under control. Instead, I focused on forcing myself to speak in tongues and give long, rambling talks about my classmates' sin in our Christian school chapel.

At Covenant College, I discovered a world of Christians who asked real questions about life and wanted to know the answers. And I discovered the works of all the Inklings, not just the few selected works of C. S. Lewis I'd found stashed away in our high school library. I learned about the man whose books would start me on the path back to the Catholic Church: Charles Williams.

I discovered Williams after reading C. S. Lewis's *A Hideous Strength*, the third book of his Space Trilogy. It's a strange book, set in 1940s England, and it's full of magic, otherworldly beings, and villains who could bilocate. I'd never read anything like it.

When I finished the book, I babbled about it during dinner to all my friends.

"I mean, come on, Merlin shows up in the book and uses animals to punish the wicked." I said, barely touching my food.

Tracy, a friend of mine with long blonde hair and on whom I carried a secret crush, smiled and said, "Have you ever read Charles Williams? I think you'd like him."

Driven by curiosity and wanting to impress her, I went to the library after dinner. I picked up the book *War In Heaven*, a modern-day Holy Grail story, and read it in two days. I wanted to know Williams's story and why everyone had the same reaction to him and his stories: they are utterly strange and weird.

Williams was by most accounts a likable, infuriating, warm, and utterly unique Christian. At one time he'd joined an order of mystical Christians and explored the boundaries of the seen and the unseen world through practicing Christian magic rituals. A confirmed High Church Anglican, he still kept trying to search for the boundaries of the seen and unseen world. He kept poking at the veil that separates the seen and the unseen to see what would leak out. In one of his novels, *All Hallow's Eve*, the poet T. S. Eliot wrote in the foreword that "Charles Williams is the type of man you want with you when you enter a haunted house. He's utterly comfortable in both worlds."

Both worlds, the idea that the physical could be intertwined with the spiritual in such a real and tangible way. As a Charismatic, I bought the idea that everything was spirit. The physical world was ignored and disdained. The Christian life was all about chasing the next spiritual experience. The life of the mind and a thinking Christian didn't exist.

Williams opened the Catholic in me, and I didn't know it. I felt the seen and the unseen worlds rubbing against each other. His book *Descent of the Dove*, a strange and beautiful history of the church, opened the idea of a sacramental imagination and thought. In one passage he quotes St. Gregory the Great: "In the hour of sacrifice, things lowest are brought into communion with the highest, things early are united with the heavenly, and the things that are seen and those which are unseen are one."

Sacrifice. Mass. Eucharist. These words stirred up echoes of my childhood, and I felt the tug toward the idea of combining the seen and unseen worlds, the rational and the unexplained wrapped up together in one faith. Williams opened doors to all kinds of possibilities.

But the Presbyterians didn't buy into that sort of mysticism, and I was looking for a place to belong. I never felt that I fit in anywhere. I loved the Presbyterian intellectual tradition and love of the arts. So I thought this was where I belonged. But the Midwestern lumberjack, mystic strain in me ran too deep to be completely comfortable.

After I graduated, I got married, went to seminary, and became a pastor of a small church in Illinois. That pastorate turned into a flaming disaster during Sunday school one day, when my inner Catholic and interest in the paranormal finally came out in the open.

"My translation says wise man."

The bald-headed elder looked up from his Bible with a grin. I'd long grown to fear a smile from this man. He didn't do it to be warm or friendly. Instead, he used it like a rattlesnake coil, a signal he wanted to strike hard and inject his venom. He ruled the roost of the small Presbyterian church I'd been called to pastor right out of seminary, aged twenty-seven. It was a church of about forty people; I soon found out why no new people darkened the door of the church for a year.

"Well, yes, that's true, many translations have it as *wise man*. But the actual word means *magos*, or magician," I said, clenching the lectern.

"Pastor, are you telling us our Bibles aren't correct?" The elder said, grin spreading over his face as he bared his coffee-stained teeth.

"Well, no, of course not. But, we've got to understand what *wise man* means in the first century. The king's advisers weren't like the president's cabinet. They had to be part diplomat, part magician, and part scientist, especially for the kings and rulers of the east. Part of their job was to consult the stars and help guide the actions of the king through reading the signs they saw there."

As I finished my explanation, the elder sat back, crossed his arms, and stared at me with the smile fixed firmly in place. Others in the room looked at one another and shook their heads. As a young pastor, I was surrounded by people who could have been either my parents or my grandparents. Some of them were very kind and wonderful people. Others, not so much. I felt like a lamb led to the slaughter.

I stumbled around for an explanation. "Well, we have to remember, we've got to take the Scriptures in their original context and audience when we try to—"

It hit me why talking about the word *Magos* was so difficult. It messed up the common story of the Wise Men visiting Jesus. We like the Christmas-play version where men with funny beards and strange gifts arrive looking like exotic politicians. For some reason, that makes us feel safe.

But call them magicians and everyone's uncomfortable, unable to cope with a stranger and deeper mystery. That is, they saw a light in the sky, read it as an astrological sign in the heavens, and came west as fast as they could. It's disturbing. Herod calls in his own wise men: magicians and the Sanhedrin. They agree the long-promised ruler is to be born in Bethlehem. Everyone freaks out, including Herod, who decides to slaughter innocent children over an astrological sign in the sky.

Dark magic, indeed.

I'd wrestled with that story in the week leading up to Sunday. The passage didn't allow me any wiggle room. The Gospels forced me to admit something about God that I didn't want to confront. If I wanted to be faithful to the Bible, I had to believe in magic. I figured that, my congregants being good Presbyterians, they would understand faithfulness to the text.

"And, we can't get around it. *Magos*, it means, roughly, 'wizard, stargazer, or soothsayer.' I know this seems strange to us. But, there is no getting around the Bible. Believe me, I tried. They were court magicians like we find in the book of Daniel. Indeed, Daniel himself was probably trained in the arts of the *magos*. Sometimes, God does things we may not be comfortable with or that meet our doctrinal criteria."

When I finished, I looked at everyone. All of them shifted in the seats and didn't meet my eyes. No one wanted to talk about this, because the implications didn't fit our traditional, Western church way of thinking. I couldn't blame them. It unnerved me too, but I decided to throw caution to the wind when I said, "I'll take it further. God used astrology and magic to announce the birth of Jesus to the Gentiles. He used things they would understand and didn't really care if it was theologically correct. He does whatever he wants to reach us where we are."

The intake of breath sucked the air out of the room. I hung my head because I knew I'd get an email that night. But I felt bound to tell the truth. While no one else was as hostile as the elder, I could tell they didn't want to hear anything else I had to say. This sort of intrusion seems to be a bit too much for them, being raised in a very black-and-white Western world, where the supernatural rarely intrudes into daily life.

But something else nagged me as I shook hands with everyone after Sunday school. I couldn't figure it out until I got home later that day. I realized that a part of me, that buried kid who wanted mystery, was thrilled that God used astrology. It went against everything I'd learned in seminary, where I'd been told that God only spoke through his word. Nothing else was needed, I was told.

As I meditated on the passage of the Wise Men that afternoon, I realized that God did whatever God wanted. God never seemed all that concerned about limits or our personal hang-ups. The world suddenly seemed stranger, wilder, and full of possibility. I felt happy and tense at the same time.

Anything might happen at the hand of such a God.

This would never square with the elders of my church or the rulers of my denomination. Everyone wanted me to be a "normal" Presbyterian who just "preached the Gospel." By this they meant that Jesus saved us from our sins so we could go to heaven. This is certainly true, but it's not the entire story of the Gospel as it is found in the Bible.

As I sat in my office, doubts poured through my head. I wondered what was wrong with me. Was I confusing people? Why did the fact that God used astrology and magic to lead the Wise Men to Christ excite me so much? Did I have an unhealthy obsession with things that weren't "of the Lord"? My love of ghost stories, magicians, and the like hadn't gone away with age. Instead, it had gone underground, though never far from the surface.

Why didn't I feel bothered about anything I'd just taught? Sure, it was in the Bible, but why did it bang at the doors of my heart and head so much? I realized then that I didn't belong with the Presbyterians. It's not that they weren't good people or even good Christians. But I suddenly knew with conviction that the Presbyterianism was not my home. I felt the tension of trying to straddle two worlds.

But where would I go? I'd committed my whole life to being a Presbyterian, with four years of seminary and my ordination trials. Sitting in my office surrounded by Protestant books, I felt as if they'd fall in on me at any moment. Loosening my tie, I resolved just to live with the tension. It would take too much to upset everything. Plus, where would I work? My whole career and time in school seemed locked up in being a Presbyterian pastor.

I looked down at my Bible with the story of the kings of the East still open. The growing anger at my situation hit me full force.

Damn Magos, I thought. *Why couldn't have God sent angels to you, so I wouldn't be in this mess?*

Mystery messes up our tidy categories. God delights in these times, because we're ready for the holy to come rushing in and burn us up in a holy fire. It's all over the Bible, people being unnerved. Angels have to tell people not to be afraid. The prophet Isaiah gets one look at God and can't even speak. St. John the Revelator stands, gobsmacked, as the real nature of the world is revealed to him in startling images of many-headed angels with tons of eyes, beasts rising out of the sea, and the talking, bleeding Lamb of God who takes away the sins of the world.

The Wise Men knew they had confronted a beautiful and terrible mystery. While they trembled, they also took it in stride. They'd been prepared their entire lives for these sorts of things.

I was not.

ORDINARY TIME I

THE WRITER: FEAST OF ST. FRANCIS DE SALES (JANUARY 24)

Jonathan

"We called you to be pastor, not a writer."

My group of church leaders in Florida all looked at me with mystified expressions, and my stomach clinched. They didn't get it, and I didn't get them. Good men, all of them, but we didn't understand one another. I couldn't speak their language because everything that fueled me was leading me away from being a pastor. I didn't know that at the time, so I argued.

"Listen, my writing is a way for my imagination to fire up for my sermons. That's how I keep myself fresh and full of life. Don't you understand that?"

They didn't say anything, but their frustration came off in waves. I didn't fit what they wanted in a pastor, and I couldn't blame them. I didn't look like the fit, trim, Lands' End model pastor of our sister church in town who wore khakis and a golf shirt all the time. When I wore that kind of thing, I looked like an angelic IT boy who might wind up on the local news with my entire name pronounced in hushed, creeped-out tones, like they do with discovered serial killers. Jeans and a flannel shirt always fit me better. Safe to say, I didn't fit the Florida Presbyterian subculture at all.

Writing had been part of my life since I was in college. Me being who I am, I would write absurdist poems with a weird paranormal vibe. The teacher took her poetry very seriously and believed I was making fun of her class. This was especially true after she gave us an assignment to write a poem based on a newspaper headline. As might be expected, I chose a *News of the World* headline, "Bigfoot Had My Baby," and wrote a poem about a mom who didn't care enough about her child, so Sasquatch had to come steal it.

Even though I'd earned an A- in the class, she gave me a B. When I asked her why, she pursed her lips, squinted at me, and said, "I feel you didn't take the class seriously enough."

I stared at her and said, "But I did all the assignments, went to your poetry readings, participated in class, and really worked hard. I don't understand."

She shook her head. "I don't think you ever will."

Confession: I still don't. I dropped my English minor, vowing never to write another word. But writing never works like that. You don't just drop it. It's a mysterious call for those of us who inhabit the written word. It bugs, it nags, it calls, it pulls, and it turns us into jerks to the people around us until we sit down to write what's in our heads.

While in seminary, I wrote out stories, ideas, and sketches. I couldn't stop myself, even as the disciples of Calvin and Geneva taught me solid biblical exegesis. When my first pastorate went to hell, giving me deep emotional wounds and probably making me unfit to pastor anyone ever again, I wrote and wrote. It was the only way I could make any sense of the world and connect with something deeper in me that was always nagging at the corners of my thoughts.

Which brings me to St. Francis de Sales.

When I received confirmation a few years ago, I took the name Peter Francis. I took the second name because I wanted to honor the patron saint of writers. He is a bit of an unusual saint in that he didn't die a bloody death, slap heretics, or become a weird bearded guy who sat on a pillar for fifty years, like the Stylite monks. In fact, St. Francis is known as the gentlemen of saints, and interestingly, the apostle to the Calvinists.

During a time when Europe was inflamed with the boil of hate, anger, and suspicion over the Bible, St. Francis became a balm of calm reason, love, and compassion. Even when he called out the Calvinists, he didn't blast them as heretics and call for them to be burned. Instead, he gently showed them their errors and invited them to come back home. He did all this through the power of his quill. While by all accounts he was an amazing preacher, it was for his writing that Pope Pius IX made him a doctor of the church in 1877.

I confess, I didn't know all this before my conversion. But, looking back, I wonder if St. Francis didn't use my writing to help me keep the search for mystery alive. As a Catholic, I've come to believe that saints do actually look out for us. And I don't think they wait until we join the church to start looking out for us.

After I left the church in Florida, I got a job as an assistant pastor in a church in Columbus. It was my third church in six years. My whole pastoral experience hit me hard in every emotional way. When I moved to Columbus, my family didn't move with me. We hadn't sold the house in Florida because the bottom had fallen out of the market. Little did I know this was probably the beginning of the end of my marriage. I can say without a doubt that my ministry experience contributed to its death.

By myself, for six months, I did nothing else at night but write. I missed my kids. And I discovered something. No one touches you when you're a man living by yourself. After years of human contact, I was suddenly without even a hug from my boys. But something kept pushing me to write.

One morning, not long after I'd moved to Columbus, I was taking a shower and thinking about my young-adult genre book. I'd spent three years writing it and it was mostly crap. The story worked, but my writing hadn't quite brought everything together. Frustrated, I decided to take my writing group's advice and write a different book. But, what to write?

As I got out of the shower, I looked out the window at the colors of autumn in full force; the leaves and grass issued the haunting call of their imminent death. Then it struck me: I wanted to write a ghost story. I wanted to tap back into my childhood, my interest in the paranormal, ghosts, weirdness, and haunting mystery.

And I discovered my main character, Aidan, who was an assistant pastor struggling with his faith. Many think that Aidan is me, but he's not, at least not exactly. His battle in my novel is over whether he will have any faith at all. Mine was never that. I always believed in God. What I struggled with was still feeling out of place, not right and not sure if being a Presbyterian fit my skin. I'll allow those struggles went into Aidan's character but only as a way to help people feel his emotional struggle.

But then, it's always hard for writers to be honest about their characters and how much those characters reflect their own lives. Truth be told, a writer is all his or her characters. They reflect exaggerated parts of ourselves or our questions about life. There is no doubt, my two 3 Gates books are reflections of my own journey toward the Mystery.

A few years before I became a Catholic, I read a book called *The Mind of the Maker* by Dorothy Sayers. Sayers presented a sacramental view of writing and writers. She believed that the writer reflects the creative life of the Trinity—that is: the conceiving of an idea, the incarnation of it through actual writing, and then the presentation of it to the rest of the world.

The parallels between the writer and the Trinity are obvious even if they're not exact. Sayers describes how writing is the incarnation of the unseen turmoil in a writer's mind and life, even if the writer doesn't want to be honest about it. And while it might be impossible for us to see what a writer's exact struggles are, they're there, on the page, in the questions they're asking at that very moment. Maybe they lie about them, but there is truth behind those lies.

As I wrote these stories, I struggled to keep sorting through the pieces of my heart and to reconnect them through the Mystery. Presbyterian theology didn't satisfy this process, because it seemed cold, limiting, and too scientific. As I connected with my supernatural beliefs of childhood through writing, I realized how much the Calvinist view of God and reality did not fit anything in the Bible or with how things worked in the world as I experienced it.

Not all, but most Calvinists avoided passages such as Genesis 6, which says that fallen angels impregnated the daughters of men. They didn't address the idea of other worlds, aliens, ghosts, and everything that spoke to my heart. I learned not to talk about my interest in these things because nobody wanted their pastor to talk about the paranormal.

The more I threw myself into seeking to integrate my interest in the paranormal stories with my faith, the more I realized that something was going on in my soul. Something stirred and rumbled and would knock down the walls that had been put there to keep part of myself separated, to keep myself safe from uncomfortable questions.

Writing, however, even nonfiction, forced me to be honest with myself. I could not deny the places opening up in me even though I didn't speak of them. In fact, I told no one. But I wrote it all in my ghost story, the glory and beauty of the seen and the unseen world. The belief that the unseen world could break through at any moment.

C. S. Lewis once lectured on his friend Charles Williams; he responded to the critiques of the novels. Williams was often criticized for mixing reality and fantasy, a common literary critique in supernatural thrillers. But Lewis turned that idea on its head when he said, "Williams began his novels by asking the question, let us suppose the everyday world is at some point invaded by the marvelous." He meant to criticize the modern notion that there is a dividing line between the closed, natural world and the unreal, supernatural world. The everyday world is the one we live in when we brush our teeth, kiss our children, or eat a burnt omelet made by our own hands. The marvelous is what hangs just beyond our sight, always tugging at us and threatening to break into our world.

For me, writing became a vehicle for the marvelous to come back into my life. It shattered the thin walls of my safe theology and safe way of doing church. The stories become my way of running from the real everyday world and toward the breaking in of the marvelous. But, when I wrote, I couldn't hide behind those safe walls.

Friends remarked on me being lost in the land of my stories. They'd ask why I often had a dreamy look on my face or why my mind seemed somewhere else. Sadly and oddly, the breaking in of the marvelous, as C. S. Lewis described it, led me into areas my ex-wife didn't want to go. She didn't like talk of the supernatural, ghosts, or the uncanny. Even though she read my stories, I could tell she never really liked them. I think they unnerved her. Every time I talked about the supernatural, she would say, "Can we please talk about something else?"

I can't blame her. They unnerved me, too. At one point, I was talking to a friend about the murder and dark magic in my book. He gave me a very concerned look and said, "Are you okay? You're really getting into some dark things. How is your walk?" A quick translation: asking about someone's "walk" with Christ is a common question among Evangelicals.

I didn't answer at first. Not because I didn't want to but because I wasn't sure myself. I thought my books and their content might be leading me down a dark path. In reality, they started to pull me out of the dark muck I'd found myself in after years of confusion, anger, and bitterness, feeling the disconnect with the Mystery, knowing it was there and trying to find it again.

Writing led me into the mystery of the Catholic Church but not before it led me through the valley of the shadow of death.

THE SKEPTIC: FEAST OF OUR LADY OF LOURDES (FEBRUARY 11)

Jessica

One must have faith and pray; the water will have no
virtue without faith.
—St. Bernadette

My daughter came home from Catholic day camp with a crèche she made from a shoebox, a St. Brigid's cross of pipe cleaners, and a plastic bottle of holy water, blessed by the deacon.

"It's not from Lourdes," the catechist told us, apologetically. For Catholics, the spring at Lourdes—dug by the bare hands of St. Bernadette at the urging of Our Lady—is the champagne of holy water. I think the batch my daughter brought home actually came from the water fountain in the school hallway. I was sitting out there with my son, still a toddler then, when the volunteers filled the plastic basin from the spout.

My own elementary school was named for Our Lady of Lourdes, and Mary was our patron and mascot to the point of insanity. My memories of Catholic education consist almost entirely of stories of Marian apparitions and miracles. Even our slumber-party games of Bloody Mary conjured images not of some demon or witch but of a glowing lady in a cave, a benevolent apparition who whispered strange terms like "I am the Immaculate Conception." One of my best friends had a small glow-in-the-dark Mary figurine. We called her Scary Mary, and I made her hide it in a drawer when I slept over.

I wasn't sure if Mary was to be feared or loved. She seemed kind enough in *The Song of Bernadette* with Jennifer Jones, the classic film about the Marian apparitions at Lourdes, but somehow I still imagined her as an omniscient scold, looking down her fine nose at me from her spot on the pedestal, condemning me and my best friend for talking too much and "refusing to come to order," as our pink demerit slips often said. I guess I thought of her as being much like my mother—kind but fierce. Beautiful and composed in a way I could never imagine myself becoming, but not to be trifled with.

Whether I feared or loved her, I definitely thought she was powerful. And I was counting on this when I told my classmates, gathered at the lunch table on the second day of eighth grade, that my mother had stage IV metastatic lung cancer. I threw back my shoulders theatrically and proclaimed that it would be okay; we were going to get a miracle. That's how I phrased it: *get a miracle*, as if miracles could be purchased at the shrine's gift shop, plucked from the shelf right next to the finger rosaries and bottles of holy water.

I can still see those thirteen-year-old girls, their forbidden lip gloss and the rumpled uniform shirts, the yarn bracelets we stacked on our wrists. I imagine a frozen Last Supper–style tableaux, forks suspended halfway to their mouths, gazes directed at one another or at their plates, all of them looking anywhere but at me. Miracles might happen to peasant children in Lourdes, Fátima, and Medjugorje. But coming from my own mouth, those words, *get a miracle*, suddenly sounded absurd. In that moment, faith came crashing down around me.

Meanwhile, my parents seemed to neither believe nor even recall the old Catholic-school stories. At home, throughout those weeks of chaos and tears and strange casseroles cooked by the neighbors, a small vial of holy water from the spring in Lourdes sat atop our refrigerator, untouched, covered with the same layer of dust as the unpaid bills and the pack of cigarettes my grandmother left behind on one of her visits.

Instead, my parents were captivated by a book called *Healed of Cancer*, by Dodie Osteen, mother of Joel, the multimillionaire televangelist and founder of Lakewood Church. Dodie had been diagnosed with liver cancer and told to go home and die, but she had miraculously lived. Not only was she cancer-free, she was healing others. We gorged ourselves on her inspirational stories. We abandoned the rosary for Dodie's favorite Bible verses, which became our new mantras.

Well, my parents abandoned the rosary. I still slept with mine under my pillow.

But those Scriptures we memorized still bob to the surface in times of need. I hear my dad whispering to us in the night, *God has not given us a spirit of fear, but of power and of love and of a sound mind.*

The Osteens called their Houston church "an oasis of love in a troubled world," and it became the spring of hope for my mother in the short weeks when hope was still possible. On one of her many pilgrimages there, she felt the heat of Dodie's hands running through her body and thought, *It's working.*

Soon we all ended up in what appeared to be a Jacuzzi bathtub sunk into the altar—no, the stage—in the First Assembly of God on the I-10 service road in Slidell. It didn't seem like too much for them to ask me to "get saved." *I'm not saved?* I wondered to myself, but it didn't occur to me to ask theological questions. I would have eaten the grass and dug a spring in the mud too, like Bernadette, if my suffering mother asked me to.

I had no knowledge of the Reformation, didn't even know the word *catechism*. I'd never been anywhere but a Catholic church and had only the barest glimmer that there was any difference at all between being this kind of Christian or that kind of Christian except that here at the First Assembly it was definitely not okay to ask Mary to get your healing.

So we waded into the lukewarm water. I was last. The pastor smiled at me expectantly, then took my hand as if leading me to the dance floor. He braced my forehead and the small of my back, and then dunked me with surprising force. I remember being shocked that he wasn't gentler with me, thinking, *I'm only a child!* I gasped and wiped my eyes as the music surged, and then, the applause.

My mother was waiting on the other side of the tub, clapping. She seemed so proud as I emerged dripping in my gym shorts.

But the world was unchanged. Same fluorescent lights. Same cheap drum kit in the corner. Same frizzy-haired lady changing the transparencies of the song lyrics on the overhead projector. Same felt banners with cotton-ball clouds. And my mother was still sick. It wasn't working. *It's not going to work*, I thought, as I sat in a folding chair with a towel around me.

It didn't work. Six months later, she was gone.

At bedtime on the last day of my daughter's church camp, I opened her holy water bottle, sprinkled a few drops on my fingertips, and made the sign of the cross on her forehead, as the catechist had suggested. "The sign of the cross is a prayer in itself," she'd said, scolding them gently for their sloppy execution. "When you make the sign of the cross over your body, you're professing your belief in the Trinity, so do it with some respect, please."

As I blessed my daughter, she looked up at me, shyly, almost embarrassed. In her eyes I thought I saw her questions. *Do you really believe this stuff?* Her credulity often surprises me, makes me wonder at the wisdom and the danger of handing on one's faith, seen but through the glass darkly, with all its tangled associations and half understandings.

Was my faith an act of love, or fear, or both?

Did I really believe?

I dipped my fingers in the water again, closed my eyes, and crossed myself.

One tiny step forward, a leap into the breach.

THE WANDERER: FEAST OF ST. PATRICK (MARCH 17)

Jonathan

I've never felt like I had a home. Not really.

In the U2 song "The Wanderer," Johnny Cash sings in a dark, prophetic baritone about wandering through "capitals of tin," sitting outside church houses and looking for Jesus. That pretty much describes my own personality and life. Good or bad, I'm not sure.

How did I get this wandering soul?

When my family moved to St. Louis, we set off a series of moves to houses, apartments, and rented property. We never occupied one place longer than two years. But, in addition to the physical wandering, I think there has been a spiritual component all along. I think that when you feel like searching for the mystery of faith, it never lets you rest. It pushes you further down the path into deeper and darker forests. You keep moving.

And yet I want to find a home, a place to belong, to call my own, where I am welcomed even when I'm at my worst. When my family left the Catholic Church for good, when we moved to St. Louis from Indiana, I felt wrenched from everything I loved, especially in the church. And it set me on a journey to find my way back. The tension of wandering through the mystery and wanting to find home became the guiding ideas of my life, especially my love for traveling.

This is why I strongly identified with St. Patrick and the Irish monks.

Just about everyone knows the story of St. Patrick (probably not his original name). He was kidnapped, enslaved, escaped, studied to be a priest, and then went back to Ireland. He preached the Gospel to the Irish, who adopted the faith in record numbers and with a burning fire.

The Irish monks turned that fire into the greatest missionary movement the world has ever seen. They heard the stories of the desert monks and wanted to live out those extremes. Except the Irish could never be alone for very long, so communities started forming. They chose the White Martyrdom instead of the red—that is, they gave up their beloved homeland to fling themselves into a boat and go where God and the tide took them. When they landed, they stayed, set up communities, and rarely, if ever, returned to Ireland, even if the home longing broke their hearts.

After my first two attempts at pastoring failed, I took up an assistant position in Columbus, Ohio. Around that time, the housing market in Florida got swallowed in the hurricane of a bad economy, poor community management, and a decline in the number of people wanting to move to the hot, humid edge of America. So, I had to move to Ohio to take the job while my soon-to-be ex-wife and the kids stayed behind to sell the house.

It didn't sell for the first month, then two, and then three. We lowered the price, but it didn't help. The strain of the situation put up walls, built up resentment, and tore at the fabric of my marriage. It also tore open wounds from my previous church experiences, of being separated from my family, and of the nagging mystery at the edge of my brain.

During the day I worked at the church, but I had my nights and weekends free. I wandered all over Ohio and discovered out-of-the-way places no one knew about. This is how I discovered the mysterious mounds.

Most people don't realize that Ohio contains some of the most interesting, mysterious, and complicated ancient earthworks in the world. We think of Ohio as the capital of "Basic, America" or a Rust Belt state that's all about manufacturing.

But just around the corner from milquetoast America, amid the urban blight and old industrial plants, are mysteries upon mysteries.

When the European settlers arrived in Ohio, they found thousands of earthen mounds dotting the landscapes. The tribes of the area denied ever making them, referring to them as "work of the old ones."

Indeed, it seems that Ohio was ground zero for some ancient death cult. In Chillicothe, Ohio, Hopewell National Historical Park preserves what is basically an enormous ceremonial graveyard. Almost directly north, at Newark, the same culture built a vast earthen observatory that dwarfs the more famous Stonehenge by a considerable measure. It's the largest earthen enclosed space in the world, encompassing a staggering three thousand acres. Many archaeologists believe that the Adena people who may have built the mounds thought Ohio was a gigantic soft spot in that veil between our world and the spirit world.

Most famous of all is the Serpent Mound in Pebbles, Ohio, the largest serpent effigy in the world. I'd heard about Serpent Mound when I was growing up in southern Indiana. So, when I found out it was only ninety minutes south of Columbus, I decided to take a Saturday to investigate it. I drove into the Appalachian foothills along the winding roads, through

Amish country to the remote Ohio state park. I told the park ranger I was interested in ghost stories and had started working on one. She gave me a strange look, checked to see if there was anyone else around, and said, "We have strange things going on here."

I raised an eyebrow. "Oh? Like what kinds of things?"

She pursed her lips and seemed reluctant to say more. I'd heard that park employees were not encouraged to talk about paranormal events. But when she heard that I was working on a paranormal novel that might include the Serpent Mound in the story, she said, "Well, it starts with the open mouth of the serpent. It's elevated and points out over a cliff, right?"

I nodded. I'd researched the mound before I made the trip. Many scientists think the wide circle valley below the serpent mount points out over an ancient meteorite-impact area.

"Well, archeologists think the ancients believed the mouth of the serpent is the entrance to the spirit world. And, well, you get a lot of New Age kooks around here saying a lot of things. But . . ."

She paused and I waited. I knew any more questions might make her shut up. "Well, we've all heard things here. Seen strange apparitions. A lot of people get sick around here."

"Sick?"

"Yeah. As in, puke sick. Nauseous, as if their balance gets thrown off."

I nodded, not sure I believed everything she said. She didn't seem crazy to me. She seemed like a normal park employee: nice, but part of the scenery.

"Well, guess I'll check it out for myself."

I started to walk along the path around Serpent Mound. I tried to adopt a skeptical stance toward the whole thing. But the more I walked, my heart pounded, and I started getting dizzy. I actually did find myself getting sick when I reached the mouth of the serpent. My heart pounded, and I rushed around the rest of the path. Once I reached my car, everything went away.

Maybe it was the power of suggestion. I can't honestly say. But the whole experience influenced the novel I wrote, and it opened up another window to the Mystery. Every time I traveled, I looked for these kinds of thin places.

The more I traveled, the more windows opened. Everything I'd tried to trap inside and keep tamed came pouring out. I didn't understand until later what had happened. But it had something to do with the ancient Christian practice of pilgrimage. It threw me out of being a "normal" pastor and into something different.

Everyone could see the struggle even if I couldn't. The people in the church I served thought I was too weird for them and encouraged me to enter campus ministry. When my wife finally moved up with our kids, I found that I'd become a different person, one she didn't understand and didn't seem to like that much.

I felt isolated and alone. No one seemed to get my explorations of the strange. In six years of living in Columbus, I don't think I made a single friend who wanted to invite me over. There were even times I felt dangerous, as if I'd somehow lead people astray with the wild thoughts roaming through my head.

The whole thing made me want to travel more and be alone. My actual home felt strange to me, and, when I traveled, I wanted to be home with my kids. I started questioning a lot of the doctrines of the conservative Presbyterian Church that had ordained me. The denomination felt confining, restrictive, and it didn't encourage the sort of paranormal exploration I'd started delving into and writing about in my novel. No one wanted to be around the weird very much.

To be honest, I didn't react to the isolation very well. In one fight, my wife said, "You want to be alone, don't you? You resent being a dad and I sometimes think you want to be alone."

Panicked, I said, "No, no, that's not true. I just, I don't know how to describe what's going on with me."

She shook her head. "Are you depressed again?"

"No, I don't feel like I am."

All I wanted was to be told that I wasn't weird, that what was going on inside me wasn't strange or that the struggles of my faith restructuring itself made sense. The problem is, I'd been so good at putting up a good front as a pastor and husband with all the spiritual answers, people—especially my wife—couldn't handle it when I didn't have any.

"Well, I think you're just one of those people who will never be happy with anything or any situation," she said. "But I need you to get over it."

I couldn't get over it, and I knew it. But I felt as if I couldn't tell her this, not in a way she'd understand. So, I shut it down. I shut down any attempts to communicate, and I tried to pretend. How could I tell her what would make me happy or would ignite me when I didn't even know?

Looking back on it now, I realize that the tension of wanting my true home and wandering around, looking for God, had begun to pull me apart. Those two desires pulled me apart because I didn't know how to sort through their seemingly contradictory feelings. I thought about the Irish monks, read about their prayers and some of their struggles. They didn't know how to resolve their feelings either. The wound of parting from the Catholic Church that I loved, that brought me close to God, and the subsequent separation from it had damaged me more than I'd recognized.

Finally, one day, the pastor of the church where I worked sat me down and said, "This isn't working out. I just have this feeling you don't belong here."

I stared at him, not really understanding. "I, I'm not sure what I've done wrong. I've done everything you asked me to do."

He shook his head. "It's not about that. I just feel like it's not working. The personalities aren't working together very well. I've talked to the leaders and convinced them. I think it's time for you to find a new job."

I was being let go because he had a feeling. I didn't know what to tell my wife, as we'd just bought a house and moved up from Florida for this job. Fortunately, I found one pretty quickly as a campus minister, but it would involve me raising all my own money, something I'd never done.

My wife didn't like it, but we didn't have any choice. We didn't want to move again, so I agreed to start raising money as soon as possible. But the inner struggles I had, the push and pull of spiritual turmoil, would not let up.

I found myself cast out on the waters, with no sail, no oar, completely at the mercy of God and the elements. My boat didn't have far to sail, as it grounded on the shores of the Ohio State University, the largest campus in America. There, I found myself ministering to one of the toughest crowds around, who certainly wouldn't share my spiritual struggles. They didn't have any, because they were atheists, I thought.

But on the island of the atheists, I found the thread that would lead me back home.

LENT

THE FIRST WEEK OF LENT

Jessica

By the time I moved to Pittsburgh, I was twenty-five, and I wasn't really a *practicing* Catholic anymore. After my mom died, my dad continued to go to fringe nondenominational churches, and technically I wasn't allowed to go to Mass, though I drifted in and out of various houses of worship, always sitting in the back, always ready to bolt.

But I still had a fascination with religion. I also marked time as a native of southern Louisiana, where Lent follows Mardi Gras. I didn't go to church anymore, but Lent was still a time to do some soul-searching, maybe go on a diet and eat fried seafood on Fridays. It was also a time to wear sandals. But in Pittsburgh, nobody celebrated Mardi Gras, it was still snowing, and I was even more confused and homesick than usual.

I didn't want to admit it, though. For the first time since my mom died and my life spun off its axis, it seemed that I was on the right track. I'd gotten a full scholarship to get an

MFA in creative writing. I had a coveted paying job as an editor of a respected literary journal. I was planning my wedding to a good Catholic boy—a Notre Dame grad, no less—who was a promising young writer I'd met at school.

So why was I so uneasy and afraid?

I wanted to elope, but Dave wouldn't go for it. He wanted a party, and besides, he said, "We're Catholic. There has to be a Mass."

Never mind that our Catholic practice at this point was limited to reading Flannery O'Connor and Andre Dubus. Dave had presented a paper on the two writers at a conference we both attended, and I'd fallen in love on the spot.

Never mind that we lived in the same house (the priest politely ignored our matching addresses when we showed up for the premarriage counseling the church requires). Never mind that he was my second fiancé and that we'd both lost count of the number of our previous affairs. Never mind all that. We were Catholic. Catholicism is what brought us together. We shared an imagination, a vocabulary, a symbol system. In a hypersecular world of humanities grad students, we recognized each other right away.

The day after our first "date," Dave and I lay head to toe on my sofa, nursing hangovers, passing a pint of peanut-buttercup ice cream back and forth and watching *The Exorcist* on cable.

"You know what my favorite part is?" Dave asked, and passed the pint. "It's when the priest says that the devil wants us to despair."

I swooned like it was the most romantic thing I'd ever heard.

So there would be a wedding. There would be a Mass.

I remember the first week of that year's Lent well, if only because I wrote it in my diary. That was the only writing I was doing, whatever I was telling everyone in my workshops.

That Tuesday my sister called to say she'd be coming to the wedding alone because her husband had to work.

I told her I understood. I was twenty-seven, old enough by far to understand work obligations and the complications of traveling cross-country for a wedding with three kids. I wasn't upset. It wasn't important enough for her to take off work. "I don't even want to go the wedding myself," I laughed, deflecting with humor, as usual.

But there was still a sixteen-year-old girl in me—the one who had to take out her nose ring and wear a ridiculous wine-velvet bridesmaid's gown to my sister's opulent first wedding in our hometown, in the church we'd grown up in, surrounded by our friends and what was left of our family—and that girl was pissed. She pounded on my heart with her fist and screamed, "You are not important!" and "Nobody loves you enough!"

I ignored her, made some excuse, and got off the phone with my sister.

But the next night, Ash Wednesday, the wounded teenager sneaked out again.

We'd gone to the evening Mass at Sacred Heart in Shady-side and had the ashes ground into our foreheads. The priest who gave me my ashes struck me as the kind of guy who could have gone one of two ways: the priesthood or the stage. He reminded me of Bill Murray in *Ed Wood*: effeminate, with a great sweep of silver hair and a flair for the dramatic. He attacked my forehead with the ashes, booming, "Remember! You are dust, and to dust you will return!" as if he were the very voice of God. He gripped my skull with his fingers and made the sign of the cross between my eyes with his thumb.

Ouch.

These were not the velvety ashes from the church of my childhood that gently dusted my eyelids throughout the rest of the day. These were black like coal and felt like ground-up bones. My eyes widened with a combination of shock and ecstasy. I considered wiping the ashes off and going back through the line.

The feeling I got from that priest's strong hand on my fore-head and his theatrical professing of my mortality stayed with me while Dave and I went home and heated up some lasagna from Whole Foods and opened the bottle of wine from the woman he'd helped when she fell on the ice on our steeply sloped street.

But after this especially gratifying Mass, nothing on TV was dramatic enough for me. I was crashing from a holy high, and it made me homesick and irritable.

Then Dave started talking about his novel again, and how he thought he'd found a way to tell the story that was not just a sex, drugs, and rock-and-roll story—"white boy fiction," as the women in our department called it. But I knew that Dave was really writing the stories of all his important and formative relationships—aren't we all?—and the sixteen-year-old suddenly woke up, with her purple hair and her nose ring and homemade tattoo, and demanded to know where she fit on this continuum.

"Where is my great love story?" She wanted to know, bang-ing again with her fists. She may be sixteen, but she's read the Brontës. She wants her Heathcliff, her soul mate.

But it's more than that.

"Why do you love me?" she wants to know, though she's never been satisfied by the answers, because she means, "*How could* you love me? How could anyone?" This obnoxious little girl is sure she is despicable and hated—because she was hated most of all by me.

She embarrassed me, because in my twenties I'd cultivated a coolness that she betrayed. I'd escaped my past. I'd left the home where people knew me as the girl who couldn't bear the grief of her mother's death, who wept in the driveway when her father drove away from her to be with his new girlfriend, who chased her first love, the altar boy, down the street screaming, "I hope you die, you asshole!" after he broke up with her for being too sad. In Pittsburgh, I wasn't the daughter of a holy roller who tried to lock her up in an institution, or the girl who attacked her stepbrother in the hallway of her high school because he told people she cried at night in her bedroom while listening to Pearl Jam and that he'd heard her begging Eddie Vedder to come and save her (all true). I was no longer the one who had panic attacks at parties, who lay on the floor in the fetal position until the ambulance came.

In Pittsburgh, I was a promising young writer and editor. I was writing a thesis about the women who worked with Andy Warhol and spent my days elbow deep in the archives of the Warhol Museum on the north side, surrounded by cold, emotionless, ironic pop art. I spent my nights in bars watching bands with other people who were so self-conscious they could barely stand to nod their heads to the beat. In Pittsburgh, I was in control. I was becoming a new person, and I didn't want anything to do with the past.

"Ugh, another dead mother memoir," a coeditor of the journal sneered while going through a pile of submissions one day.

"Yeah," I said. "Enough already."

That Thursday I came home from work to an empty house and was instantly worried. This was before everyone had cell phones, but Dave usually called me at least once every afternoon from the office he shared with all the other adjuncts at the university, and he'd talk so softly that I was always asking him to repeat himself, or speak up. He never had anything to say. He just called because he could. Sometimes he'd read me a paragraph or two of something he'd written or something that he was reading. Or he'd tell me that he had band practice. Or he'd ask for a ride home. Or he'd ask if I needed a ride home, if he'd taken the car we were sharing. He'd linger on the phone, and I'd grow impatient.

But I hadn't gotten one of those calls, and now the house was empty. Where was he?

I turned on the TV and saw that *Twin Peaks: Fire Walk with Me* was on IFC. I picked it up about halfway, when Laura Palmer is just beginning to suspect that her dad may be a shady character. She is in her bedroom, preoccupied by two framed paintings. One is obviously creepy: it is just a cracked door in a dark hallway. The other is classic Christian kitsch: a family gathered around a table with an angel standing at the head keeping watch. While Laura watches, the angel disappears from the picture.

I hadn't seen this prequel since I was in college, and I was struck by how heavy-handed it all seemed, when I used to think it was so cryptic and cool. I was so sure that I had everything figured out. Why, with every passing day, was I becoming less so? Why, if everything was going right, did it feel as if I was going in the wrong direction?

Every so often I checked the phone to be sure it was plugged in and that I hadn't missed a message.

Where was he?

I told myself he was fine. He always had band practice on Thursday nights. Surely he'd be home soon.

But there she was, my inner teenaged self with her shrill, hysterical voice, a Mickey's Big Mouth Lager in one hand and a bummed Camel Wide in the other.

"He's never coming home!" she shouted. This is one of her favorite taunts. She loves predicting my sorrows.

I talked out loud to myself—Grow up, already! Dave is probably having a great time playing his trombone and smoking pot in downtown Pittsburgh. You've got to get over this idea that every time you say good-bye it will be your last.

It made Dave crazy, the way I was always saying, "Please be careful." I said it a lot back then. I said it with eyes wide and hands gripping the sides of his arms. Not just when he was going out of town for the weekend with his band to play a show, or to go to an old friend's wedding. I did it even if he was just running out to get a newspaper or to pick up another six-pack for a party we were hosting.

The little departures are almost worse. Wouldn't it be awful to think I lost him for a Sunday *New York Times*? For one more Dos Equis with a lime? The sixteen-year-old knows all too well: it would haunt you for the rest of your life, that you let him leave without one last important moment where you looked each other in the eye.

There was a time my mom left me home alone to go to the grocery store. I was sure I'd be fine, and I was, for about an hour. I played records on my dad's stereo and danced in the living room. But when she left it was afternoon; soon it was getting dark, and she still wasn't back. I started to feel sick that I had insisted that she go alone. I would be forever responsible for what happened to her, and I was suddenly sure she was dead. I felt certain there had been an accident. By the time she pulled up in the driveway, I was sitting on our front porch, on the little wooden bench with the heart cut out of the back, and I was hysterical, crying and sweaty and snotty. It turned out that she'd stopped at the fabric store to buy Jennifer and me some more yarn for the friendship bracelets we were into making back then. I was so mad at her for scaring me that I never made another bracelet again, and every time I saw the yarn in the little yellow plastic bag I felt sick, the way I would feel when she told us she had cancer, the same lurching feeling, like vertigo.

So I performed my superstitious little ceremonies in which I said the right words and touched Dave the right way, as if blessing him. As if this warning or this appeal—"Please be careful"—followed by this charm—"I love you"—could protect him.

I know this sounds like classic OCD. (It is classic OCD; I have a diagnosis.) These were the same sorts of compulsions that made me crazy as a kid—the same things that made me think, when my mom really did die, that I'd had a sixth sense about it. That I'd always known she would. But how psychic is that? Of course we know that everyone will die one day, that it is just a matter of time until the day that someone leaves and doesn't come home. There's nothing so intuitive about that. It didn't even happen the way I thought it would. She wasn't yanked from me by a trip to the grocery store. It took a year for cancer and chemo to claim her.

It was not really the revelation of death that tormented me, but my obsession with the revelation. Was I the only person in the world who was aware that we were all dying? Clearly, I was not. So how did other people ignore it so easily? What did people do to distract them from certain mortality? How can we say good-bye for even a few minutes when we know that we are all going to die? That one day it really will be, as Jeff Buckley sang in one of our favorite songs, our last good-bye?

The next day was the first Friday of Lent, and on my way to work that morning I walked past Sacred Heart again. I saw the kids filing in and realized they must be going to the stations of the cross.

When I was in Catholic school, we prayed the stations of the cross during the last part of a Friday afternoon, the last bit of the school day before going home with a friend or to a slumber party, or to a Lenten fish dinner with my parents and grandparents at Thonn's Restaurant on Pontchartrain Drive. I remembered it was painful—so much kneeling and standing and kneeling and standing—and boring, and because it was painful and boring, it was considered a penance, and penance earns you a bit of grace, a blessing.

I was already late for work, but I decided to duck in the back and watch.

I don't know what I was looking for or expecting to find—maybe the thrill I'd had on Wednesday with Father Fabulous. But instead, I found in that sanctuary the memory of myself before my mother's death changed me. I saw myself as the child who didn't yet know grief, not the sixteen-year-old girl with all her open wounds.

There I was, quiet and intimidated in second grade, checking out the older kids with curiosity. And in fifth grade, giddy with tweening, whispering to my girlfriends and growing so fast, taller than all the other kids and slouching to hide it. And in seventh grade, sitting next to my first love, close enough to feel the heat of his body, careful not to touch. By eighth grade the plaid skirt is an inch too short, the feet too big on the skinny legs. The boys have the beginnings of acne and greasy hair.

I was overwhelmed by the smell of them, the scent of childhood—my childhood: incense, sweat, the smell of outdoors, of recess.

Once they were all settled in the pews, one of their teachers stood in the front of the church and called them to attention by saying, "Let's practice." And then she hummed the refrain you sing between the stations, the Stabat Mater.

And that's when I lost it.

The Stabat Mater or, in my bad translation, "The Standing Mother," is considered one of the greatest Latin hymns of all time because of its simple, plaintive melody and what I've heard described as its devotional "sweetness," though only Catholics would describe a hymn about Mary standing at the foot of her dying son's cross as "sweet."

The hymn has been in liturgical use for centuries and is taught to Catholic schoolchildren as the hymn of the Way of the Cross, sung as we process from station to station, entering the agony of Mary and Jesus as they both walk toward certain death.

> At the Cross her station keeping,
> stood the mournful Mother weeping,
> close to her Son to the last.

The stanzas change with every verse, but the tune is the same. It has the simplicity of a nursery rhyme, so it's easy for a young voice to master, but it's the saddest song I've ever heard. I hadn't prayed the stations of the cross in fifteen years, and those little voices singing the grief of the world—the inevitable procession toward heartbreak and loss—hit me like a wave hits when you're not ready to dive in and ride it. It knocked the breath out of me, and I sat and hid my face.

Two of the older kids read the text for each of the stations. They flanked the priest in front of the altar. They probably rotated every week, or maybe only the best readers got this honor. That was how it happened in my Catholic school. These kids were good readers, but how can a twelve-year-old wring the right kind of painful humility from Psalm 118?

> I lie prostrate in the dust; give me life according to
>   your word.
> I declared my ways, and you answered me; teach
>   me your commands.
> Make me understand the way of your precepts, and
>   I will meditate on your wondrous deeds.
> My soul weeps for sorrow, strengthen me with
>   your words.

I was in tears. I often was. But these were not tears of despair.

Hearing all these young voices enunciating Scripture in unison, I remembered a feeling that I'd long forgotten. I suddenly felt overwhelmingly connected to my past, to the living and the dead, to nature and super-nature. I wouldn't say it felt like I was home; it was not a feeling of finality, of arrival. It was more that I could see home again in the distance, and knew I had discovered the right path toward it. It was a feeling of grateful anticipation, of having suddenly picked up the trail again when you were sure you'd be lost forever.

This is why I'm a writer, I thought. It's not because of Warholian detachment and irony. It's because I see symbols and metaphors and poetry—and yes, death—everywhere. It's because I learned to love the rhythm of words when I memorized these prayers and hymns and when I dipped my head and bent my knees to the kneeler.

This was the day I became a practicing Catholic. I know that because I've been going to Mass and devotions such as the stations of the cross ever since. But it's also the day I really became a writer, because I finally knew my material. I've been wrestling with grief and faith on the page ever since.

But in the moment, I barely had time to digest the experience. I'd remembered these fourteen sections, the hours from Gethsemane to Calvary, taking a little eternity. But this Passion was over in forty-five minutes. It had barely begun when it was over and all the little ones were hopscotching from brick to brick all the way down the center aisle and out the double doors.

I had to wait a minute with my head hung low, dabbing at my eyes while the big kids single-filed out, teachers shushing them as they whispered and giggled.

I walked on to work, thinking again of that angry, heartbroken girl I'd been running from. Only now, I didn't hate her so much. I wanted to love her. I wanted to hug her and brush her hair and paint her nails, to invite her to stay. To give her a home again at last.

The rhythm of the stations stayed in my head all day. It was the first Friday of Lent, and Dave was leaving to play a show as trombonist for the Mekons in Detroit. I had a craving for fried seafood, so we met for oysters in Pittsburgh's Market Square before saying good-bye on the corner of Fifth Avenue.

Priest: We adore you oh Christ, and we bless you.

Genuflect.

All: Because by your holy cross, you have redeemed the world.

I made the sign of the cross over the car as he drove away.

HOLY WEEK

Jonathan

I stared at the screen, cursor blinking, unsure about what to write. How, I wondered, do I tell people I want to build a campus ministry around atheists, Christians on the edge, malcontents, science nerds, and all the people larger campus ministry organizations probably would reject? None of them were the beautiful people or campus leaders who would influence the influencers, as they like to say in the ministry books.

This fact got driven home at our first meeting of what we called the Thomas Society, named after the famous St. Thomas, who wanted to put his fingers in the wrists and side of the resurrected Christ. A reasonable request, in my point of view.

As the kids gathered, some wore *Star Trek* T-shirts, others sported long beards, obscure indie rock T-shirts and nose rings. I seriously doubted anyone would include them on a ministry brochure, which are usually filled with Ken and

Barbie Christian with a token black, Asian, or Hispanic person thrown into the mix to look "multicultural."

I used the first meeting to explore what sort of questions they wanted to discuss in our group.

"I want to know about why Christians can't see the pagan roots of Christianity."

No problem, I thought. History and theology are in my storehouse of the brain.

"What about suffering? Why does God even allow that? Is he cruel?"

Nodding, I understood that one too, knowing there were very few answers to this question that would completely satisfy.

"Science. What about science? Doesn't it disprove Christianity? Hasn't the church always been hostile to it?"

Caught. I'd never been very good at science. Certainly, I'd thought about science and faith issues only on a very superficial level. But at the same time, I love geology, walking in nature and spent a lot of time looking at the stars. However, science always seemed to be a cold discipline, ready to threaten people's faith at a moment's notice. I knew in my head this was not the case, but I felt the threat. To equate science with wondering and searching for the mystery is not a connection I would have made.

But now, as I looked at all the college kids in front of me, I would need to explore that further. I'd need to know a lot more about science. I didn't believe in evolution, having been taught it contradicted the story in Genesis, but I also didn't buy into a seven-day creation idea either. Beyond that, I couldn't explain the issues of science and faith very well. I would need to spend a lot of ministry preparation time reading a ton of science or science-related books.

That didn't bother me, but how would I write about that in my ministry letter? Ministry fund-raising letters are supposed to be full of "awesome" things, "decisions for Jesus" or kids who "made a deeper commitment." No one would want to hear about the long arguments about evolution, the historical Jesus, or how these kids loved to argue about the most minute point of theology.

And, with each question they asked, I started to confront my own inabilities and limitations. These kids stretched me into areas I knew nothing about nor could I ever hope to know. I began to see that my resources, as good as they might have been, weren't enough. I needed to find more information on topics such as the Big Bang, evolution, science, and everything the modern atheist considered important. They would never take me seriously otherwise.

I dove into my science reading. I started with the history first, finding out that Galileo didn't really get persecuted by the church, at least, not in the way that is normally presented in popular culture. In fact, the Catholic Church has, throughout history, sponsored huge scientific discoveries. Not being Catholic at the time, I had no vested interest in this information. It just surprised me to discover some of this history.

The list is impressive and includes Pascal, Copernicus, Pasteur, Mendel, Bacon, and the priest who proposed the Big Bang theory, Father Georges Lemaitre. I read modern Catholic scientists who convinced me of the scientific fact of evolution and the idea that it didn't conflict with the Christian faith. So, I had some answers for my students.

What I didn't expect was that this historical research would introduce me to the wonder and mystery of science. It made me think deeply about the wonders of nature that surrounded me. Since they knew that I loved atheists, the Secular Student Alliance, the national atheist student group, asked me to be on their speaker's bureau. They paid for me to travel to any of the student groups who wanted to hear a Christian preacher speak to a bunch of atheists.

The student group at UNLV asked me to come to Las Vegas. Even though the group sounded great, I didn't have any desire to visit Las Vegas, which I knew only as city filled with gambling and prostitution. Still, I figured, it would be an experience.

I didn't want to hang out too much in Vegas during my downtime, so I looked for a state or national park not far from the city and found Red Rock State Park about forty miles north. I decided to take a drive.

About twenty miles out of the city, civilization disappeared. The landscape stretched in all directions, with very few houses or gas stations to get in the way. I marveled at the time it took nature to shape that land, giving it its color, texture, and contours.

When I got to the park, I found a hike that would take me away from the main roads of the park. Large red rocks rose over me as I walked into the canyon, and silence engulfed me. No airplanes flew overhead, I could hear no cars and no conversations. Complete and utter silence. Then, I looked at the red rocks, which took millions and millions of years to form, to have their ragged beauty shaped. I realized that these mysteries of creation were far more compelling—and they pointed more effectively to the artistic mysterious nature of God—than if God had created them out of nothing in six days. The longevity of this place invited me to think about the mystery of the world.

I encountered petroglyphs that were at least a thousand years old. I wondered about who made them and why, and what mysteries they contained about the lives of the people who created them. It struck me then that my narrow brand of Christianity couldn't hold that sort of mystery. It needed something bigger.

Or smaller. Around the same time, I started reading about quantum physics. The more I read about the quantum realm, the more I thought about the Catholic position about the body and blood of Christ transforming the bread and the wine. As a Calvinist, I'd been appalled by the idea. Christ's body is at the right hand of the Father, and it couldn't be anywhere else. Only his spirit could be present in the Eucharist. Science, Calvinists, believed, didn't allow for that sort of thing.

But quantum physics tells us a different story. As it turns out, reality as we know it doesn't work in the way we've always thought. As Professor Stephen Bar once put it, "In short, one can explain the doctrine of transubstantiation and distinguish it from other beliefs about the Eucharist without any use of the Aristotelian apparatus. I don't know what quantum mechanics has to do with any of this. If anything, quantum mechanics makes a straightforward connection between what appears empirically and what is 'really there' more obscure than it was in Newtonian physics, and to that extent would make it easier rather than harder to affirm the doctrine."

It made me think of what Jesus really meant when he said to his disciples on Maundy Thursday, "This is my body and this is my blood." Martin Luther believed that Jesus meant what he said. And so did many other Christians.

That train of thought led me into a realm I didn't expect. What started off as a means to answer my rationalistic students led me into thinking about the deeper mystery of reality. The idea that God could be bodily present and in other places the same time, such as in the Eucharist. Indeed, the Resurrection suggests a new fundamental reality that science might be only beginning to understand. The seen and unseen worlds blend with each other so well that, sometimes, we can't tell the difference.

On a particular Maundy Thursday, I decided to attend the parish a block from my house. My marriage was almost completely done, and an unknown future stretched out before me. Everything I'd known about myself—gone and destroyed. I didn't know what the future would be or how I'd even go on.

I could face none of it and walked into the Catholic church. To be honest, I don't remember much of the foot-washing service or any of the details. All I remember is, when the priest elevated the host and said, "This is Christ's body, broken for you," I really believed it. And I knew I'd have to come back into the church, not knowing what that would mean for a job, my future, or anything.

All I knew was, I wanted to go home.

I wish I could say a miracle happened after I reentered the church that February. That my family got fixed and we're all happy Catholics now.

Sometimes, in this sin-sick world, the happy ending doesn't happen. Instead, my wife got a job in St. Louis, and I got a job in South Bend. I didn't have much of a choice, as no one seemed eager to hire a guy who'd spent sixteen years in a ministry job.

"It doesn't seem you've got any marketable skills at all and certainly not any that would fit this position," one potential employer responded.

But I knew how to write and edit. Eventually I found a job at Ave Maria Press in South Bend, Indiana. After moving my kids to St. Louis, I trudged up north with what little stuff I had. The grimy and gross apartment welcomed me into its disgusting arms.

That first night, I sat in the living room, staring at the ceiling. I looked around at what would be my home. The carpet was a light gray that didn't hide dirt very well. With only two lights and two windows in the apartment, the place didn't get much sun. It felt like a jail cell.

Only a few months before, I'd lived in a beautiful house surrounded by my kids. I could sit on the porch and read as I watched them play with their friends. I could watch the trees move in the wind and say hi to neighbors as they passed on the street.

There, though, I sat alone with no friends nearby and no one to grab for a movie. Everything had gone to hell, and no light shone into my heart. I thought about death. I identified with the Psalmist who wrote in Psalm 88:

> My couch is among the dead,
> like the slain who lie in the grave.
> You remember them no more;
> they are cut off from your influence.
> You plunge me into the bottom of the pit,
> into the darkness of the abyss.

I'm pretty sure the only reason I never seriously considered suicide is the Eucharist. Every Sunday, I would force myself to Mass, not wanting to go and just wanting to sleep. But I would trudge to the mystery. Often, I would pray to die. When I told someone about this, they said, "What about your kids? Don't they prevent you from wanting to die?"

I looked at them, coffee cup in hand, and I said, "You don't understand. I think they would be better off without me."

It was only the Eucharist—the mystery of eating Christ—that kept me bound to life.

One Sunday, I knelt at the Consecration of the Host and listened to the words of the priest:

> Take this, all of you, and eat of it:
> for this is my body which will be given up for you.
> Take this, all of you, and drink from it:
> for this is the chalice of my blood,
> the blood of the new and eternal covenant.
> which will be poured out for you and for many
> for the forgiveness of sins.
> Do this in memory of me.

My brain went to a strange place. I thought about a song, "Chop Suey," released fourteen years before by the band System of a Down. According to the lead guitarist Daron Malakian, it's a song about how we all deal with death and horrible things.

But what's most interesting is that, in the middle of the song, lead singer Serg Tankian sings out in a heart-cracking voice, "Father, why have you forsaken me?" And then adds other bits from the Psalms, "In your thoughts forsaken me. In your heart forsaken me."

It's a beautiful and startling piece of theological observation about Christ's cry of dereliction on the cross. SOAD uses good old-fashioned Jesuit imagination by putting themselves in Christ's place to imagine what he felt. The band always stated they put those lines in there for a reason but never explained why. From the context, it's clearly meant to tie Christ's feeling of abandonment with those who feel the same way at the time of crisis or death.

I thought about that song and realized that I felt the confusion and anger it conveyed. Prayers poured out as I screamed at God in my mind, "Why? Why me? Haven't I always tried to serve you? How did you let everything go wrong? What's your problem? Why did you abandon me to the darkness?"

I didn't get an answer, but I thought about Our Lord. Why did he say those words? I tried to imagine what he felt: the pain, the agony, the utter desolation. Then I remembered a time when I was a kid: I lay across a piece of railroad tie and tried to imagine what Jesus felt. That didn't last long because I felt a creeping darkness I couldn't identify.

Why? Because, at that moment, when Jesus says those words, the Second Person of the Trinity is separated from the Father and the Spirit. They could not bear to look at him because the sin and shit of the world covered Christ.

If I hadn't been kneeling already, my knees would've buckled. The Mystery grabbed me. When Christ said, "My God, My God, why have you forsaken me," it wasn't just a cool psalm-quoting moment in which Jesus winks at the camera and says, "Get it? See what I did there? I fulfilled prophecy!"

Of course, that seems silly, but that's how some theologians have tried to explain away these words. I find that sort of explanation odious because it takes away from the power of the moment: God *divided*. God blaming God for this terrible situation. God laying the blame on God for the state of the world. God taking punishment for God.

This seems to be a new idea, but it's not. God told us he would do it this way. He gave us ideas and pictures. When he put a rainbow in the sky after destroying the earth through a flood, he put the blame of the world on himself, aiming his own battle bow towards himself. How do we know this? In ancient Mesopotamian culture, the bow was a sign of the gods going to war. From what I can see, God is telling us that God will go to war with himself over the condition of the world.

We get further confirmation of this in Genesis 15. God wants to make a covenant with Abraham in a way that he'll understand. So God orders the patriarch to cut the animals in half. Again, in the culture of the time, this was a common ceremony between king and vassal. Basically, the vassal pledged his service to the king by walking through the blood, bile, sinew, and muscles of the cut animals. The message being very clear: you break this covenant with me, and this is what will happen to you. Talk about effective visual communication.

Abraham probably expects to walk through those cut-up animals. It would make sense. He would understand and accept the facts—that is, any covenant breaking would mean ole Father Abraham becomes food for the buzzards.

But that's not what happens. Instead, God walks through the cut animals. God takes the curse of any covenant breaking and the consequences.

As I prayed through the Our Father, I thought about the mystery of God's separation and how Christ embraced that darkness for us. The pain, the loneliness, and the feelings of betrayal. All the things I'd been feeling for the first few months of living in South Bend.

I didn't get any real answers, not the ones I wanted. I wanted to know why, but we're never really told why. When we come face-to-face with the mystery of the separation of God at the cross, it blows our minds, questions, and categories. And it replaces them with a longing to know more.

The beauty of it is, God doesn't stop the questions; he invites them. In the book of Job, when he appears on the scene, God rebukes the friends of Job who offered such uninformed theological observations. He lets Job question all he wants. And when God appears on the scene, he tells Job, "Okay, you've had your time of questioning. I've heard you. Now, it's my turn, because this is a conversation." God answers Job's questions with more questions. It's not a "sit down and shut up" moment. Rather, it's meant to be an invitation to go higher and deeper into God's mysteries. Oddly, at least for us, Job seems comforted by it. He realizes there is more going on than he can see. It's a moment of wisdom and deeper contemplation.

The loud bang of kneelers shook me from my thoughts with the invitation to receive the Body and Blood of Christ. As I walked down the aisle toward Father Tom, I realized that I'd been in pieces my whole life, torn apart because I'd left the Catholic Church. Convinced of my own ability to take the Bible and figure it all out, I'd spent years convinced that, with the Bible and God, I would be able to get to the bottom of my theological questions.

But maybe we never get to the bottom of theological questions, perhaps not even in heaven. Maybe the mystery of faith is meant to be a training ground for heaven and what it will be like. Maybe now we're practicing how to accept that we can't and won't know everything.

It's at that moment that I think I understood what it means to be a Catholic. All the pieces of my life started to reassemble, centered on the mystery of God's separation and suffering. God suffered. He understood what it meant to take on and feel pain, misery, and isolation.

Sure, it's a cliché to say that misery loves company. But it's also true. When we mourn, cry, and throb with our own pain, we don't want to be alone. We seek people who know what it's like. We seek God when we're suffering, but under our breath we mutter in sarcasm, "Sure, like you know what it's like. You're God."

The mystery of Christ's cry says otherwise. It's an invitation for us to draw closer to him and give our own cry of desperation and separation. It occurred to me that this is why Catholics emphasize suffering so much. It's not because we're masochists who love pain but because we know this is where we can find and contemplate the mystery of God. That's where we can begin finding answers, as well as new questions.

How? I have no idea. That's the mystery of it. As a minister, I would have given a ton of pat, theological explanations. But, in the face of real suffering, none of them matter very much. As I took the Body and Blood of Christ, I knew it was time to live into the Mystery that had beckoned me since I was a kid.

I needed to learn how to be a Catholic and stop running from God's mystery.

I needed to embrace the full-on otherness of my faith.

EASTER

EASTER VIGIL: TO THE TOMB AND BACK

Jessica

The summer before Dave and I got married, he went away to teach at the Governors School for the Arts, a program for brilliant young writers, and I stayed behind in our rowhouse in Pittsburgh, trying to finish my master's thesis, which I still hadn't started. I knew I could no longer write a collection of profiles of the women who worked with Andy Warhol, but I hadn't broken the news to my thesis director yet. I had to turn in my first draft at the beginning of the new school year.

One night, there was a terrible thunderstorm, and my friend Rachael came over to keep me company. We drank mint juleps, and she read my tarot cards while the storm knocked the trees into the windows like in a horror movie, the air charged with electricity and meaning.

I don't know all the secrets of tarot reading, but I remember that if the image on the card is upside down, it means something—something about blocked potentiality, abilities, and events that want to manifest but can't.

She flipped the first card. It was upside down. So was the next. And the next.

All my cards were upside down.

I was secretly terrified of playing at tarot. The words "dabbling in the occult" came to mind. But I was ashamed to tell Rachael for fear of sounding like a fundamentalist nutbag. I've always been excessively religious, and I watched too many horror movies at too young an age. I knew from *The Exorcist*, *Rosemary's Baby*, *Witchboard*, *Fright Night*, and others, that it starts out as fun and games, and then suddenly you realize that Captain Howdy is the devil and your neighbor is a vampire.

My older sister was braver. She spent years searching for a way to connect with our dead mother. She sat for past-life readings, trained herself to achieve a hypnogogic state that would allow her to fold space, and meditated in something called a psychomanteum—a form of mirror divination—in attempts to contact our mom's soul. It was while sitting before that mirror, in the back room of a hair salon in Dallas, staring at her own reflection for endless quiet minutes, that she says she came to her senses.

What will I do if she shows up? she thought. After all those months—years—of preparation, she couldn't think of a thing to say. So she walked out, got married, had three babies, and started teaching aerobics.

I'd begun to feel it was my job to keep the search for our mother alive. If her ghost was out there wandering the moors, somebody had to keep the window open. I couldn't write like a Brontë, and I didn't have my Heathcliff. But maybe I could *be* Heathcliff.

At the time, Dave and I lived in an old house on the edge of historic Homewood Cemetery, which, given my squeamishness about the supernatural, should have disconcerted me. I remembered *Poltergeist*, and Craig T. Nelson screaming, "You only moved the headstones!"

Nonetheless I found it strangely comforting to be on hallowed ground. I loved the place. It was a great neighborhood, home to families, not grad students like me who smoked on the porch all night. Our backyard rolled into an expanse of soft green lawn, thickets of trees and crosses and angels and the occasional spray of flowers. At night, hundreds of red votive candles flickered in the darkness like a celestial event.

I watched funerals reflected in the bathroom mirror as I brushed my teeth. I marked how quickly the grass grew on the fresh mounds. I began to recognize the mourners who came regularly. I watched them stand beneath umbrellas in the misty rain, their maps unfolded and flapping in the damp breeze.

In Louisiana, where my family is buried, you have to put people in crypts and tombs and mausoleums, or they will wash away. New Orleans is below sea level, and the ground is saturated, unstable; bodies decompose more quickly. I used to imagine floodwaters carrying the bones off in the tide, or my mother's body floating down Canal Street toward the Mississippi River, her hair fanned out like Ophelia in the famous Millais painting.

But in Pittsburgh, only the very wealthy are buried in vaults: the Fricks and the Heinzes and the Mellons. They rest in Millionaire's Row, section 14, near the lake. In the summer, a guided tour called "You Can't Take It With You" takes groups through section 14 every morning before it gets too hot.

Many mornings I woke to the sounds of riding mowers and men shouting over the repetitive tones of something large backing up: Beep. Beep. Beep. Breaking new ground back there, space for more bodies.

If I didn't finish my thesis by the end of the fall semester, I'd join the ranks of the many in our graduate program who never completed their degrees. For three years, I'd been honing my techniques as a journalist or cultural critic, researching the women who worked with Andy Warhol, to write a collection of *New Yorker*-style profiles. Pittsburgh is Warhol's hometown, and I'd moved there to track down his family, his church—the Byzantine Catholic St. John Chrysostom—and to work in the archives of the Andy Warhol Museum, to rifle through his Time Capsules wearing white gloves.

I had pages of transcribed interviews with Pat Hackett, his secretary and the redactress of the Andy Warhol Diaries, and I'd just been introduced to Gerard Melanga, the guy who did the whip dance with the Velvet Underground, who agreed to talk to me about Warhol's relationships with women (for $1,000). I didn't have $1,000.

But the truth was, the more research I did, the less interest I had in Warhol or his women. I was spending more time in church than at the museum, sitting in the dark of Sacred Heart in Shadyside, though still in the last pew just in case I needed to make a hasty escape.

The only thing that really fascinated me about Warhol anymore was that he went to Mass every day. What could have attracted Warhol—known for his cold detachment, his voyeurism, his straight-up *weirdness*—to daily Mass? My friend gave me a reproduction of his painting of *The Last Supper*, and I spent hours studying it instead of writing.

I also spent hours in the psychology and religion section at Barnes & Noble in Squirrel Hill, sitting in a chair by the window overlooking Murray Avenue and wondering if I should have been a therapist.

"I understand people," I told Dave over the phone during one of our nightly arguments. "I'm intuitive."

I also wondered if I should have been a high school teacher or a librarian or an archivist—or anything besides this. Whatever *this* was. A grad student not writing her thesis, watching people pass on Murray Avenue two stories below, haunting a graveyard like some teenage goth.

"Give yourself a new project," Dave said, yawning into the phone. He was in Erie, three hours north of me, teaching fiction writing and drinking wine with a poet who lived next door to him in faculty housing. They played surrealist bocce, whatever that was, on their lunch breaks. Whenever he'd been teaching, he had an annoying habit of treating me like one of his students if I complained about writing, and it was really starting to piss me off. I'll never forgive him for telling me to cover my laptop screen with a towel—a method he used to help students write more freely. But he has always approached writing with more realism and practicality than I have.

I have always wanted to be a mystic.

"Well, then. Make something happen," he said.

I hung up on him and jammed the box fan into the open window and stripped down to my underwear and lay on the bed, on top of the covers, feeling sorry for myself, crushed by the weight of my unwritten thesis and a grief that I couldn't believe was still so hard to bear, when my mother had been dead for more than ten years.

If I could just find some way to exorcise it, I thought, I might be able to write—if not about Warhol and his women then something, anything. But whenever I tried to write, my stomach hurt and I couldn't breathe.

So, instead, I walked the paths behind my house, memorized the names on the graves, left flowers, and tried not to think about the only grave that really mattered, alone and untended back in Louisiana. I flipped idly through bridal magazines, trying to get excited about the wedding I was planning. I took fitful naps and had nightmares.

I dreamed that I presented my thesis to my committee. I opened the box where the manuscript should have been, and instead, there was an ornate tomb carved in stone, with a bust of a woman's head as a sort of finial on the peak. My thesis director carefully placed the thing on the conference table and walked around it several times, shaking her head.

"It looks nothing like her," she said.

When I woke, it was dusk, quiet except for the echo of a basketball on the pavement, ticking away the minutes until summer would end and Dave would come home and my thesis would be due and my time would be up.

Make something happen, Dave had said.

I remembered my sister and her psychomanteum and thought, why not? I imagined building an elaborate contraption, pictured myself in the basement working a table saw, wearing a pair of safety goggles.

I thought I'd get at least a chapter out of that.

But when I found Dr. Raymond Moody's book *Reunions: Visionary Encounters with Loved Ones*, I learned, with great disappointment, that this stunt required nothing more than a mirror, a comfortable chair, and a dim light. One man reported that his mother actually stepped out of the mirror and hugged him. He says he picked her up and lifted her clear over his head.

The psychomanteum is a tool of divination, like a crystal ball. I told myself it was as harmless as reading my horoscope or having my fortune told. Something a Victorian might have done at a spiritualist tea-party séance. A game. And the world's most clever writing prompt. Charles Dickens and Thomas Edison both used to induce trances when seeking inspiration. So did guitarist Jimmy Page. Visionary states enhance creativity. Altered states of consciousness enhance perception, inspire new ways of understanding.

And many people believe they bring you closer to God. So there.

But what if I saw something I didn't want to see? In *The Odyssey*, hundreds of spirits appear to Odysseus before Teiresias finally emerges from the pit and gives him directions home. Moody never quite says it, but the subtext is clear: you might get nothing, and you might get something bad. Something evil.

Then there's this. The spirit might not appear while you're in the psychomanteum. She might appear in the rearview mirror, sitting in the backseat of my car the next morning. I tried not to dwell on that scenario.

Then I tried to think of my one question. Moody says this increases the chances for success—benevolent success. The question might go unanswered, or the spirit might answer a different question altogether. But it was important to come prepared.

I'd come back to that. Surely, I'd think of something.

All day I marked pages with Post-its and made notes. As the sun set, I stalled and reread book 11 of *The Odyssey*. While Odysseus is in the pit channeling spirits, I imagined my own story winding around his like a caduceus. Odysseus didn't call the pit he filled with blood, milk, honey, wine, and water a psychomanteum, but it's the same concept.

I'll pray for protection, I thought. I'll bless the ground with holy water. I was afraid. I was also ashamed.

Because really, it wasn't a stunt. I wanted it to be true. I wanted to summon my mother from Hades and free myself from grief. And if that was too much, I hoped that this project would at least bring about some much-needed change in me, supernatural or not. Like my sister, who walked away from her search, left the mirrored room, and went on to marry her true love and give birth to three babies and get on with it.

In ancient times, there were elaborate sunken caves and desert oracles. All I needed was a reflective surface and a comfortable place to sit and think. I'd make the sign of the cross and burn frankincense to ward off evil spirits. I'd surround myself with her memory—play Stevie Nicks's *Belladonna*, spritz a bottle of Giorgio, chew a pack of peppermint Carefree.

I'd wait for twilight, for the crack in the spirit world to open, and I'd sit and gaze beyond my own reflection, and remember.

Dr. Moody says there are only two guarantees: (1) whatever happens is what needs to happen, and (2) if I work hard enough, something will be revealed.

But when I lifted my head from the notebook in which I'd been frantically scribbling those notes, the spell was broken. The bookstore came back to life around me, the din of a dozen or so grad students flirting or clicking away on their laptops, the coffee grinder whirring, dishes clinking in the bus bin. I packed up my books, pens, and Post-its and headed out of the café and onto Murray Avenue, feeling jittery and foolish.

It was warm, a late-summer night. The sun had set, and I was too afraid to walk home alone past the cemetery in the dark, so I was turning back to Barnes & Noble when I heard my name in the dimness, and my heart jumped. In a moment, Dave's form emerged in the light from the streetlamps and the shop windows. He was walking toward me, smiling and waving his hands, jingling the car keys.

Surprise. I'd conjured the living.

That October, on a beautifully crisp and blue-skied fall day, Dave and I got married at a historical Catholic church near his parents' house in Ohio, followed by a quiet reception in their backyard during which I drank too much champagne and Dave watched the Notre Dame–Purdue game with his dad.

I was far from home, and there were so few people on the bride's side of the church I felt embarrassed, but in the end, I was grateful that Dave had made me go through with it, even though I'd tried to back out right up until I walked down the aisle.

I'd grown so accustomed to funerals, I hadn't realized how happy a wedding could make people. I felt buoyed by their love and good wishes, borne aloft into the future.

A couple of weeks later, on Halloween, trick-or-treaters were bused to our street from Pittsburgh's rougher neighborhoods to collect candy from our porch. We drank beer while our friend Brandon brought the bowl down to the smaller kids who couldn't manage the steps, or to those who were too shy to come closer. He was always a natural with kids. He helped me imagine our children in the world years before they arrived. My daughter and son call him Uncle Brando.

In the backyard, the votives flickered on the graves in the dark. A new memorial was complete, an elaborate temple with Doric columns, a eulogy engraved on a plaque: she was an artist and a teacher. She accepted people for who they were. She was shy as a child and socially sophisticated as a woman. She had a positive self-image.

So oddly formal and yet so personal—"socially sophisticated"? But then, as if her parents had gotten halfway through their polite eulogy before throwing down the chisel and crying from the heart: *We knew the real meaning of grief when we no longer could see your bright face!*

It wasn't exactly poetry, but it was a run at the gates.

Back inside the house, I collected the pages of my thesis as they emerged from the printer, started telling the stories of my life, stacking my grief like stones.

PENTECOST OF THE WEIRD

Jonathan

When I returned to the Catholic Church, most people didn't understand. Some people thought I was giving a finger to my years as a Protestant. Others thought it was my rebellion before, during, or after divorce. In other words, instead of dating twenty-five-year-olds, getting a sports car, or showing my chest hair, I bowed the knee to the pope.

Most people thought it was just plain weird. One day, I tried to explain everything to a friend. As I told her my story, her face slowly descended into frank disbelief. Finally, I stopped and said, "What?"

She wrinkled her nose and said, "But, don't you think Catholics are kind of weird?"

I stared at her for a moment. "What do you mean?"

She fumbled around and said, "Well, I mean, no offense, but I don't get why you became Catholic. I mean, eating Jesus? Cannibalism? The Mary thing? Praying to the saints?

It's all kind of bizarre and strange; did you really think about it before you reverted or converted, or whatever it is?"

The truth is, I'd thought quite a bit, but maybe not enough. I shifted in my seat.

"I mean, it all seems a bit pagan, don't you think? Sacrifice of Jesus? Lighting candles? Bones of the saints? Christmas being a pagan holiday and all that? And what about praying to Mary?"

For a moment, I tried to deflect by saying, "Well, you know, I'm not *that* kind of Catholic . . ." I stopped myself. What, I wonder, kind of Catholic am I? For a while, I tried to describe myself as an evangelical Catholic, like many of the former Protestant ministers who'd gone on before me. But that never seemed right either, as if I were trying to hold on to some semblance of respectability with my friend.

I struggled with how to explain it. And then, I thought of that blessed Protestant "saint," C. S. Lewis, who is still one of my favorite writers.

"So, you remember what happened with C. S. Lewis's conversion?" I said.

She shrugged and furrowed her brow. "A bit. I remember the motorcycle ride to the zoo."

"Right, but do you remember the convo he had before that with J. R. R. Tolkien and Hugo Dyson on a late-night walk?

They talked about true myth, how Christianity is the fulfillment of all the pagan dreams. Tolkien pressed the point pretty hard. He wanted Jack to see that just because pagan religions had stories similar to Christianity, that didn't mean Christianity wasn't true. The opposite, in fact. Indeed, if you think about it, if Christianity is true, and God promised what he did to Adam and Eve, wouldn't it make sense to see the story of Christianity through the rest of world history? It's the story that all other stories copy of that grand, divine narrative."

My friend nodded, waving her hand, "Yeah, yeah, I got it. I like that argument for the truth of Christianity."

"Yeah, me too. But, there is more. Think about it. Tolkien was making the argument. He was a Catholic. He'd argue that Catholicism was the fulfillment of paganism, and by that I mean old-school paganism. That is, burning Beltane fires, decorating trees, or whatever else. It's the full-on baptism of the imagination and good, pagan practices. The Jesuits adopted some of the Native American cultural practices in their Masses, for example. They knew Jesus fulfilled all the old stories, so why not show everyone how this worked through using their own cultural practices? To be sure, many times this was done at the point of a sword. But most of the time, old-school pagans dropped their old beliefs for Christ. Many people accuse Catholics of co-opting pagan practices and integrating them into the church. And, I realized from Tolkien's argument that Catholics should shrug and say, 'So?'"

My friend stared at me for a moment. "Guess I hadn't thought about it that way."

I shrugged. "I hadn't either. But, you're right, Catholics are weird and pagan in the best sense of that word. To me, that's a good thing. And, to be honest, I'm still embracing that and yeah, it's a little weird."

It is still weird for me to be a Catholic. Everything seems strange, and I know it looks bizarre to people outside the church. Like me, most Catholics know this and often try to distance ourselves from the strangeness of it all. Nowhere is this struggle more evident than at Catholic Disneyland, Notre Dame.

On one of my first nights living in South Bend, I decided to walk on the campus of Notre Dame. It's a beautiful campus with stone buildings, beautiful statues of Christ, the Blessed Mother, and various saints. The Grotto is a popular place to gather and light prayer candles.

But, at the center of it all, at least to me, is the Basilica of the Sacred Heart. When you walk into the church, it vibrates with old-school Catholicism. There are tombs in the church, a huge relic collection of saints, complete with a wax child in repose. At the top of Mary's head are two boxes of her bones. This, to me, is Catholicism at its most weird.

At the same time, it looked like a normal university with students going about their business. They all looked like decent, productive citizens who companies drool to hire. Indeed, they all seemed to be the fulfillment of the American dream, and one wonders if Catholics finally fit into a country that never wanted them. The theme of course, is God, country, and Notre Dame, the school motto.

Everywhere you walk on campus, you can't help but think about respectable Americans who are striving to make their country great through their academic excellence. They look like people who wouldn't challenge the notion of loving their country. America changed the church and started to take out the teeth of its prophetic call. If you couldn't kill the Catholics or drive them out, blunt their witness to the mystery of faith by making them fine, upstanding citizens.

The need to be wanted and liked runs deep in our history. This is understandable. When Catholics started to come to America, they faced prejudice from Protestants. Bizarre rumors floated around about aborted babies buried at convents and evil priests out to lead astray the chosen of God. No one in America really wanted Catholics around. Everyone thought they did weird stuff, said weird stuff, and challenged the authority structure. This continued throughout history until John F. Kennedy, the first Catholic elected president, had to swear up and down he would not take orders from the pope. In 1960!

Now Catholics try to fit in other ways, and this can lead to strange discussions. I'm on parish council at a church that used to be known for its wild, hippie reputation. The sanctuary certainly has the feel of the 1970s. The altar area looks like something out of a *Brady Bunch* reject set. I'm sure everyone back then thought the church looked "hip" and "groovy, man."

Father wanted to redo the altar and give it a more traditional look. The discussion went like this:

People under sixty. "Yes, please, it's rather awful. If you add shag carpet, it would look like something from *Austin Powers*."

People over sixty: "This is the way it's always been, we want to leave it."

Both sides argued from the standpoint of what would make people more comfortable during worship. The wise way Father answered both sides was to engage an architect and a historian trained to work with sacred spaces. One of the wisest pastoral moves I've seen.

We all asked what would appeal to people, and Father wanted to know what was more in line with the teaching of the church. After hearing the church historian, I was convinced of the more traditional route. I wanted more candles, more statues, and more saints around the altar. The more I thought about it, the more I realized why: it brought everything under the Mystery of Faith.

When I first came over to the church, I didn't make the connection. I came over for three reasons. One, I believed in the Catholic Church and its apostolic authority stretching back to the apostles. Two, I believed the Eucharist became the literal body and blood of Christ. And three, I was an emotional wreck and the church felt like a great place to recover.

But everything else was an alien world to me. Lighting candles, praying before relics, asking the saints to pray for us, and Mary, oh Mary. I could not get over all this Blessed Mother business. The strain of being a Protestant for most of my life died very hard.

Still, the Mystery called to me. I figured out why I became a Catholic again—the real reason, the one that motivated my heart. Catholicism embraces all the weird and the strange. Ghost stories? Yeah. Apparitions of the supernatural? Of course. A full embracing of the idea found in the Nicene Creed when it tells us that God is the creator of all things, seen and unseen.

I understand why Catholics want to fit in to the American life and not be considered weirdos. I tried my whole life to fit into cultures that didn't seem to want me. I'd run the gamut from a Charismatic speaking in tongues to a hard-core Calvinist who loved to talk about the most obscure points of theology. I never fit. Many people thought I'd drift into liberal Protestantism, but that didn't fit either. Nothing fit me except the weirdness of Catholicism; it contained the mystery I'd been searching for my whole life. It brought all the pieces together.

Then, as I made my way into the church, it seemed as if everyone else wanted to leave. Even at Notre Dame I started meeting Catholics who wanted to get out of the church, who were already out, or who had stopped attending Mass. It seemed as if the entire church had colony collapse disorder, like the ones destroying all the bees.

It didn't make any sense to me. How could everyone want to leave the mystery? And I soon realized: not everyone felt the same way I did. In fact, very few people felt the same way. Ex-Catholics are one of the largest denominations in the United States.

As an editor at a Catholic publisher, I find myself in this discussion all the time. What does losing all these people mean? What will reach new people? How will we get new readers and new writers with young people leaving the church in droves? Why are they leaving? Lots of theories abound on that one. We think the church is outdated in its worship practices, social hours, and its unwillingness to make church more convenient for people. Or, we think the church's teachings are outdated and irrelevant.

People have not lost their interest in spirituality. If you don't believe me, you should check out a dating website sometime. A friend of mine showed me the profiles of all the women he found. In the spot marked "religion," they either had "freethinker" or "spiritual, but not religious" as if somehow that phrase was self-explanatory. And it's not just the women. The men do it too. So, what's going on? We've forgotten the drunken weirdness of St. Peter during Pentecost and the baptism of pagan culture by St. Paul.

Imagine the scene at Pentecost. You're going about your business in a Jerusalem market, bargaining, feigning anger at the high prices until the merchant, equally feigning anger, decides to lower it. You both feel like you got the better of the deal and you part ways, satisfied.

Suddenly, a strong, driving wind hits the house just in front of you and fire starts appearing in the house. You wonder what the Moses is going on when suddenly a bunch of men and women stumble out into the streets babbling like Jakob on a night when he's had too much new wine.

Everyone watches these people stumble around with looks of amusement, alarm, or disgust. They start whispering, "Good grief, they're drunk."

But you get closer to listen, and you realize that these people are speaking in a variety of languages. The reason it sounds like babbling is because they're speaking Latin, Egyptian, or some other language you've never heard.

And, then, one of them stands up on a pile of grain sacks, laughing a bit, and says, "Hey, we're not drunk. It's a bit too early for that sort of thing, don't you think?"

This, of course, is how Pentecost went down. Weird, right? The strange fire of the Spirit inviting people into an "other" life. People will think you're drunk. People will think you're crazy. People will think you're blasphemers and cannibals. All accusations they hurled at Christians whose strangeness was so disturbing that people killed them for it.

But that strangeness changed the world because people liked it. They came to Christianity not because it was the respectable thing to do. It challenged them, hit them, and sometimes made them angry. But it kept to the strange "otherness."

They took that "otherness" to the rest of the world. St. Paul laid it out on Mars Hill when he addressed the most educated pagans in the world. He pointed out how religious they were and that this was a good thing. But they were worshipping only shadows, he told them. Instead, worship the light that cast the shadows. In this, Paul set the stage for the Catholic Church to baptize not just individual pagan people but pagan culture itself. And for the fire to blaze on all the hilltops of Europe.

And I wonder, can we baptize our culture again by embracing more of our weirdness? If so, how?

ORDINARY TIME II

THE LUNATIC: ST. JOHN'S NATIVITY

Jonathan

Sometimes, I wonder if I was born to being strange like Job was born to trouble.

My birthday is June 24, the feast day of St. John's nativity, one of the only three birthdays the church actually celebrates (Mary and Jesus being the others). The guy wore a hairshirt and ate locusts and honey. He exuded strange as he went around the countryside baptizing people and warning them the kingdom of God was coming.

The day before, June 23, is known as St. John's Eve. In many countries, St. John's birthday is celebrated on this day, because it's closer to the pagan solstice, around June 21. During pagan times, they celebrated this date by lighting bonfires and throwing all-night celebrations. So, when the Christian missionaries arrived in these countries, they didn't really discourage the practice. Instead, they taught them about

St. John, the one who lit the fire in the darkness to be a beacon of the Lord's coming.

As a Catholic who writes supernatural thrillers, I'm amazed at the interest in all things strange, weird, and scary. People can't get enough of it. A year ago, I gave a talk at a Protestant conference called "Weird Fiction as Sacramental Practice." I talked about how strange and supernatural fiction are ways for us to explore the part of our world that is seen and unseen.

"See, the Eucharist, for a Catholic at least, is the ultimate expression of this idea. We have what's seen, the bread and the wine, being transformed by the unseen, the real presence of Christ. And, in that way, Christ can change and transform all reality, because all of reality belongs to Christ."

To my surprise, I couldn't get out of the room after my talk. People wanted to talk about this idea, that we could baptize the world through the strangeness of Christianity. I shouldn't have been so astonished.

Our culture has become what C. S. Lewis called "The Materialist Magicians." That is, we love science and all things we believe it can "prove." We also love ghost stories, spooky things, and paranormal discussions. Movies, books, and T.V. shows are flooded with the fascination of all things unseen, whether it's the new version of *The Exorcist* or the continued popularity of Stephen King.

What is even more interesting to me is that the Catholic Church, with all our bizarre history, is primed to address this culture both from a scientific point of view and by addressing the culture's renewed interest in the paranormal. The irony is, right at the time the Catholic Church should be embracing the weird, we keep trying to be normal. That pushes us further away from the people we want to reach in the pews and outside the walls.

This is why I think it's time we go back to the blazing fires of St. John's Eve and the sacramental nature of our weirdness. Or, as the Jesuits call it, seeing God in all things. St. Ignatius told this to all his early Jesuits. It's not unique to him by any means, but he really hammered it home and made it a hallmark of Ignatian spirituality.

It's this idea that I cling to when I talk about embracing Catholic "otherness." We need to come back to this idea that the world really isn't just what we can see; we need to avoid falling into the Enlightenment mind-set that often grips our culture. Everyone—not only those of us who struggle with it consciously—becomes ripped apart by trying to compartmentalize and keep separate these two realms. When Catholicism is functioning as it should, it keeps its foot in both worlds. It sees the world and reality through the Eucharist. Everything is transformed by Christ's living presence; therefore, we must seek that presence in all things—the normal and the weird.

We need to do this because it is best for loving ourselves and loving our neighbor. When I divided myself by leaving the church and the sacramental ideal, I soon fell into confusion and darkness. I felt torn in half without being able to explain why.

I'm fully convinced that our American culture feels the same. People know they are beings who are seen and unseen. But we've torn ourselves from this reality by embracing science as the be-all and end-all while neglecting our hunger for spiritual experience. We've been taught by the spirit of this age to think of them as two separate and incapable realms. We've also learned not to question why that must be the case.

I became a Catholic because I wanted to stop being torn in two. My knees knelt at the altar of the church because I became convinced that this seen-unseen tension the church holds explains all reality and stitched me back together.

While we need to be careful about making our own personal experience, I believe our culture and the church are in the midst of this turmoil. In the Catholic Church, we've backed away from the charism of the weird, centered around the Mysteries of Faith, bones of the saints, and other acts of popular piety.

In the Harry Potter books, there is a scene that breaks my heart. Harry finds the mirror of Erised (*desire* spelled backward), and it shows him what he wants more than anything in the world: to know his dead parents. If we stood that mirror in front of our culture, we'd find that the deepest and most desperate desires are grounded in this tension between the seen and the unseen. We ache for the mystery. We ache to be reminded of something other than what we see in front of us. Not because the material world is evil, but because it is incomplete. It is only part of the equation.

When my heart was split into two, I still believed in Christ, but I could never make everything connect to my entire life. I motored along like a car full of a mishmash of junkyard parts, picking and choosing from what I thought best or was the most biblical. Coming back into the church, I felt as if all my original parts had been restored.

Just up the road from my apartment is the convent of the Sisters of Perpetual Adoration. They have a chapel where the Eucharist is displayed twenty-four hours a day. You can go for adoration and sit in the presence of Christ.

Every time I go, I still feel the tension. I sit in this chapel, often with prayerful nuns, and I feel out of place. But the more I focus on the Eucharist and the presence of Christ, the more this feeling falls away. Time seems to stop, and I feel as if I'm sitting beyond time and space. The distinction between heaven and earth is no longer a valid picture of the world. This strange beauty is how things should and would be, a glimpse of an eternity filled with Christ, saints, friends, and other creatures I can't even imagine.

The more the church emphasizes this reality, the more likely people will want to hear what she has to say. We will no longer be like everyone else. We'll go back to the days when everyone thought Catholics were strange, blasphemers, and idolaters because we worshiped the real presence of Christ.

When we start talking about beheaded saints, fires in the night, and the stigmata again, the mystery returns. And when the mystery returns, we will be startled by how many people ask questions about this strange but compelling life of ours.

As I move into the second half of my life, I hope God will keep making me an agent of his weird presence, an evangelist of the strangeness of the Trinity and a proclaimer of the downright bizarre communion of the saints.

THE MEDIUM: THE EUCHARIST AND ALL SAINTS (NOVEMBER 1)

Jessica

In high school, after my mother died, I loved the song "Ouija Board" by Morrissey, which would have made my secular-music-and-occult-fearing dad apoplectic. It's just a silly and maudlin expression of the desire for connection, but I confess it still makes me cry, just as it did then. He asks the Ouija Board, "would you help me?" He needs to make contact with an old friend. He feels lonely and displaced, and his friend "has now gone from this unhappy planet."

I remember listening to that song, lying on my mom's empty bed, my dad away at his soon-to-be-second-wife's house or at some of the multiple church events he attended weekly, and feeling like Morrissey sang my deepest futile longings. I wished it was that easy. If only there was a way to get a response, to make contact. If only she would speak through a medium. If only I could put the planchette to the board and reach out for her again. If only I could build a psychomanteum or a portal she could walk through.

But in the end, this is all only a fantasy—a good story. Despite my attraction to them, I never had much faith in those things apart from their ability to entertain me or keep me awake at night. I didn't believe in magic. I didn't have much faith left at all. I just lay on the bed and listened to Morrissey and cried. I had no way to make sense of what my life had become, or to stake out the path forward.

My dad had taken me away from the Catholic Church at a time when I desperately needed its theology of suffering—which says that human suffering can be a locus of God in this world, and that, if and when we suffer, we are brought closer to union with Christ.

And it was just that easy, because the Catholic Church—at least the church as represented by my parish—let me go. Nobody came to convince us to stay—not the priest who'd married my parents and baptized and confirmed me and my sister. Not my godparents. Not my teachers. It seems strange to me now that there was no resistance to our departure from the only world I'd ever known. Maybe we bore the stigma of the family whose house the angel of death had not passed over.

And so my dad immersed me in a world where grief and anger were seen as demonic, where my depression was seen as a "rebellious spirit" at a time when I needed more than ever to hear that the grieving were blessed, not possessed.

Sometime around Halloween, I shared this Morrissey song with my friend, a poet named Joanna, and told her about how I used to long to be able to make contact with my mother. She wrote back to tell me some unnerving experiences she'd had with a Ouija board:

> I am a freshman in college home for fall or winter break. The board is still at my house, and I've decided to play with it by myself. I soon find that it does indeed seem to be pulling toward different letters. I contact an older male family friend, a grandfather figure, who died when I was in fourth grade, and the planchette spells out, "Can I just say, you have grown into quite a lovely young woman." This is not something I imagine saying about myself, and I'm struck by the lack of economy, the conversational quality of it. It sounds like a voice, not my own. Still, I can't discount the fact that maybe this is my subconscious telling me what I want to hear. But there's more.
>
> Later, I am speaking by phone to the guy in my dorm who I am seeing (before later falling for a mutual friend of ours and spending the next three and a half years with him). I am at the kitchen phone in our yellow house in

Leavenworth, and I ask this guy, who I will call Jack, if he has anyone dead he wants to contact because I am now a medium! He says he'd like to contact Tom, a friend who had killed himself in the dorm the previous year, an understandably traumatizing experience for Jack. So, I cradle the phone with my shoulder and contact Tom. I tell Jack to ask me something only he and Tom would know. "Where did we go for Tom's twenty-first birthday?" he says. The planchette spells out, "H-U-N-A-N." Hunan? What does that mean? Human? "No," says Jack. "The Hunan restaurant. That's where we went." I had never been to this restaurant and didn't even know what it was. Tom then spells out, "Tell Jack to watch *Conan*." "*Conan!*" Jack exclaims. "We loved that movie! We had a tape of it and watched it all the time." Later that day, Jack called me back to report that he had watched the *Conan* tape. "Yeah, so, at the end of the tape . . . there's Tom. *Conan* had been recorded over a tape of Tom just talking and joking around. It's like he was saying hello to me."

While I was reading Joanna's stories, I heard a loud noise in the next room. When I went to investigate, I found a framed picture had fallen off the wall and lay on the floor, unbroken.

I'm sure it was just a coincidence.

My religion is more than campfire tales and slumber-party tricks, though. I promise. My faith isn't just about poking a stick at the unknown, though I admit I like that aspect very much, the idea that the seen world teems with the unseen, and that, on both sides of the veil, our actions impact each other. But really, the Catholic Church—for all its reputation as a hidebound rulebook of patriarchal oppression—was the only place I really felt I could come as I am. In the kinds of churches my dad went to, my ongoing struggles with grief and depression disqualified me from Christianity; if I was still suffering, I was clearly doing it wrong. And my attraction to mystery was also a spiritual deficit—a dangerous curiosity.

My dark imagination—which I came by naturally but certainly wasn't helped by encountering death at a tender age—was not a liability in the Catholic Church. What my dad saw as morbid, I saw as a reflection of the reality I was living. This was something I sensed, not something I was told. It was why, after my mother died, even though I wasn't allowed to go to Mass, I found myself seeking refuge in Catholic churches. I'd slip in the doors, light a candle, and lie in a pew.

Immediately after Dave and I married, we moved away from Pittsburgh's plentiful, dark, incense-heavy, and nearly empty churches, and I had to contend, for the first time in my life, with Catholicism outside a catholic culture. A Catholicism that felt foreign to me, because it was utterly disenchanted.

At our country church in rural Virginia, I was shocked to see they kept the holy water in an old Gatorade bottle. But at least I was in the South, on recognizable ground.

Then we moved to northern Michigan.

Up north, I felt completely unmoored. The land was unrecognizable: a monochromatic moonscape of rocky beaches and frozen lakes and evergreen forests. And the Catholic churches I found in rural northern Michigan didn't seem any more set apart from the flow of time than their social halls did. No more could I seek refuge in an ethereal world of hot wax and flickering light, melt into years of other people's faith in a place where death has no sting. They smelled not of holy smoke but of food and musty carpet and HVAC systems.

At our first Mass up north, the parish priest thoroughly shocked and horrified me when he described stained glass and art—both lacking here—as distractions.

My dear man, my inner Chesterton bristled, *that's exactly why I'm here.*

So instead of the pews, I began to find myself in the pine and cedar woods, searching for a place that was ancient and undisturbed. This, northern Michigan has in abundance.

I walked fast, headed nowhere, looked for God shining in a break in the trees, on a bluff, or on a dune that gave way to a glassy lake like a portal to another world.

And I drove six hours south to Chicago as often as I could to visit my best friend and go to Mass with her at one of my favorite sacred spaces on earth, the German gothic St. Gregory the Great in Andersonville.

During such a visit on All Saints' Day (during our first year in Michigan), I wanted to be sure take a picture of the Pietà, one of St. Greg's many shrines, this one to the Mother of Sorrows, who bears the swords in her heart. Another woman approached, and I backed away to give her space, watched her as she lit a candle and then reached for Jesus' cold, slack hand, the hand of a dead man cradled in his helpless mother's arms. She gave it a calm maternal squeeze, as if she were the one comforting him.

When she moved on, I got pictures of the shrine with my phone. It felt unseemly, but I needed a souvenir to remind me when I returned to the north that there are still places like this in the church, not just in my memories, and not just in my books. Places that are built to hold our pain and unite it with something larger. I lit my candle and let my sorrow flicker there with all the others, released it like a fish in the water.

Back in Michigan, I had only that picture. But it was something. I looked at it often to remind me of what was real when I felt like the ground was shifting under my feet.

I was desperately homesick, for where, I didn't even know—where was home anymore? I felt betrayed by my husband, who'd moved me away from a landscape and a house and a community I loved. I felt betrayed by God, who I felt had revoked what I'd seen as my reward for years of grief and sadness: a place that had become home, the place where my children were babies, the place where I wrote my first books.

I stopped going to Mass. Without Catholicism to ground me, I lost my constant—the one thing that always felt familiar.

One morning I proclaimed defiantly to myself that I was going to be a nature-worshipping pagan. It was a steely-skied November day, and I remember I had dropped my son off at preschool and was sitting in my car by the bay, listening to NPR, a seagull crying on my parking meter.

Instead I decided, on a whim, to go to eucharistic adoration at the church downtown.

Adoration is the Roman Catholic practice of exposing the Eucharist, the consecrated host that we believe is the body and blood of Christ "hiding" under the "Eucharistic species," and sitting before it in quiet contemplation, or adoration. It's old-school piety that's made a comeback (or never left) in many more traditional parishes.

When I arrived at the chapel—a tiny room off to the side of the sanctuary of a hot-mess post–Vatican II church-in-the-round—there were several people there, kneeling in silence, and I felt awkward shouldering my way in with my heavy bag full of extra clothes and *Star Wars* toys and a half-eaten banana. I sat. I settled my body as well as I could. I listened to my own loud breath mingling with theirs.

This was not St Gregory's, with all its intricately carved wood, imbued with years of incense and tears, prayers whispered under the shadow of two towering sinewy archangels bowing before a gaunt crucified Christ. This chapel was not beautiful. It wasn't even chapelish. Really, it was almost offensive to me, with that mass-produced Divine Mercy tapestry with the laser beams shooting from the heart of Jesus, the slogan "I trust in you" in a corny script across the bottom. The white noise machine on the wooden table in the corner was just a little too mundane a reminder of my own bedroom. I chided myself for needing something more than this to imagine divine love.

If I loved God better, I fear, I wouldn't need transcendent chants, a dead language, or prismatic stained glass that obscures the present tense with stories from the swirl of history and the promised, longed-for future. But my starved heart and overfed imagination need help to conceive of a love that is both like what we've known and yet far greater, ever-lasting, eternal.

But sitting there in that ugly chapel, I began to come to terms with my aesthetic longings, to subjugate them to my need to be near what is truly and unfailingly holy: the Eucharist, the small circular wafer, the host in the ornate monstrance on the tacky little table.

To be an art-loving, art-making Catholic today is to struggle against the worst of the banal, the ugly, the artless, every single Sunday and then some. So I'll plug my ears and put out my eyes and feel blindly for the altar.

This was not the first time I'd found myself at adoration in the midst of a crisis of faith, or a crisis of life. When I think back, again, on my teen years, those years of feeling homeless in every way, bereft of mother and home and church, I mostly remember a dark road. When I turned fifteen, I got my driver's license and, with the (very) small sum of money my dad gave me after he sold my childhood home, I bought myself a real beater of a car that you could hear coming from blocks away.

I didn't want to go home; my dad had remarried and had a whole new family and a new house and a new faith; I felt like a stranger there. This is why I was always driving. Gas was less than a dollar a gallon then, and although I usually couldn't afford dinner, I could always scavenge enough pennies and nickels to get a few more miles.

Sometimes I'd pick up another kid I saw walking on the roadside. My hometown was like that then; I felt like I knew everyone. Even when I didn't, if they were of a certain age and dressed a certain way—flannel, the right concert Ts, piercings—I could bet I knew someone who knew them. I made a lot of new friends that way. My old friends—the friends I'd grown up with—were part of another universe by then, one from which I'd been expelled by personal tragedy. There was an awkwardness between us now, too many moments when none of us knew what to say. I needed friends like me, I thought. Friends who didn't have to be home for dinner.

It was on one of those long, aimless nights that I ended up in the chapel of St. Margaret Mary. Perpetual adoration was going on, but even though I'd been raised Catholic and had gone to Catholic school my whole life, I had no idea what eucharistic adoration was. I don't think I even knew the Eucharist was there. But I liked that the chapel was quiet and candlelit and safe. It felt like home. It felt familiar, like my mom. I signed my name in the little book at the back of the church and sat in a pew. The chapel was empty and dimly lit. The only noise was the air conditioning rattling on and off. The air smelled of spent matches.

Sitting in that chapel made me feel safe. It gave me a place to step outside my life. And I really do believe it sustained me on this lifelong journey toward faith and relationship with God.

In adoration, there is no pressure, no set prayer, no knowing when to stand, sit, kneel. There's no annoying youth pastor trying to be cool and win your trust. There's no youth programs that pander to what they think young adults want. There's just presence.

The psychologist Lisa Miller's research suggests that, during the teen years, along with a surge in hormones, there's an increase in capacity and desire for connection with others and with God. Teenagers, far from being less interested in communication and relationship, are "propelled like clockwork into an accentuated hunger for transcendence, a search for ultimate meaning and purpose, and the desire for unitive connection." That explains so much to me about who I was as a teenager: desperate to unite with something greater, something more.

As a teenager stumbling across the lights at St. Margaret Mary, I couldn't believe my dumb luck at finding such a refuge, a place that was beautiful and secure, where the doors were always open. Now I see it as grace. I remember being alone there, as I remember being alone for most of those years.

Now I know that someone else must have been there, that the host is never unwatched. But in my memory, it was just me and God.

Somehow, that chapel with its open doors—open to me even in the middle of the night—stayed with me on the dark roads. I never forgot it. I always knew I could come home to the Catholic Church and eventually, as an adult, I did.

And again, in Michigan, I think it was daily adoration in that little chapel that not only kept me Catholic, but also kept me alive. I was suffering through the worst bout of depression in a lifetime of major depressive episodes. I didn't know who I was anymore. I had no energy for prayer. I was discouraged by Mass in these churches that only brought back memories of houses of worship where I'd never felt welcome. But every day, after dropping my son off at the (Catholic) preschool, I'd go around the corner to the little ugly chapel and sit, often for only five minutes, with the host. Sometimes I cried openly. Sometimes I read a book—not a theology book, any book. And sometimes I prayed. But not always. Sometimes I just let myself sit there with Jesus and—at the risk of sounding crazy pious—let him love me. The priest at St. Gregory's had given me that advice: "Just sit quietly and let yourself be loved by God."

I kept going to Chicago—six hours south—as often as possible, to rest in liturgical beauty and the love of my best friend and godchildren. I even arranged for my daughter to make her First Communion there, because it felt more like home to us than anywhere else.

It took me two years to join a parish in Michigan. And when I did, I joined the choir and signed up for all the ministries. I dove in and made myself go every Sunday. Slowly. So slowly. I began to feel I belonged there.

It is not a beautiful church. Many of my fellow parishioners find me strange. But I keep going because they say God is there. *I* say God is there. And the brass monstrance on that awful tapestry holds all of heaven, every soul who ever lived, every moment of experience, every beloved breath or soft patch of skin, hidden not in a bottle of dandelion wine but in a wafer of bread.

Because no matter how ugly it gets, how conflicted I feel about my place within this tradition as a woman and a weirdo, there is no more seductive promise to me than this Eucharist, the only real shot I've got at leaving behind my sworn enemy, time. No, I can't quit this church, even if she stubbornly abandons or forgets all the other ways she offered escape from the relentless grind of the everyday that wears all things down to dust. Without the Eucharist, I'd be left to books, ghost stories, and fairy tales, lost in the north woods, searching the cedar cathedral for a place where I can read God's language again.

I still do—sometimes. I walk in the woods at night and marvel at the clarity of the stars, the looming terror of the enormous evergreen trees. But at this point in my life—a forty-year-old woman with two kids—I've tried almost every possible way to manufacture the numinous, from the New Age to the neopagan to witchcraft and mediums and call-in psychics and past-life readings and, yeah, even that brief flirtation with mirror divination.

None of it worked.

I've begged to be haunted, but I've never even felt my dead mother's presence with me, unless I'm listening to Stevie Nicks, and I think that's only because my mother loved her so much that some part of me believes Stevie Nicks *is* my mother.

I don't dabble in the occult anymore because it didn't work, and because I've found a better way.

Christianity makes wild claims, and Catholicism makes the wildest and weirdest of all: bread that becomes flesh, rituals that break into eternity, saints who roost in trees and fly from their caskets. For me, it's the only place I feel I can truly and rightly worship.

On All Saints' Day, I arrive early and spend some time alone in the choir loft with the pipe organ, admiring from my perch the darkness below, the candles, the little table of relics—tiny bits of saints' bones and blood encased in sparkling golden frames, reliquaries—that the priest had lovingly arranged in front of the altar.

My nails are still painted black from Halloween night, and my temporary bracelet tattoos of skulls are just beginning to peel from my wrists. This seems right. A month of spooky tales and ghost stories has prepared me for this feast. And the darker side of my imagination and experiences—my goth and my grief—led me here, to the Catholic Church. We sing the Litany of Saints as the priest and the altar boys process to the altar, following each name with the plea, *Pray for Us.*

Calling out to the dead, asking for a response.

"We are here, surrounded by spirits," the priest says in his homily. He points out that the schoolchildren dressed as saints are an external sign of a hidden reality. The saints are here, now, and at every Mass.

"We are all pilgrims," he went on, "and this church is our ship. We are on our way to another land." But he didn't mean that we won't arrive in that strange kingdom until we die. We need not wait for eternal union with God, or for reunion with those we grieve. "When we process to the altar, we leave time and enter eternity," he said. Every time the host touches the tongue, heaven and earth meet.

"You have made contact," he said. "You have communicated."

EPILOGUE

Jonathan Ryan

It's been more than a year now since we launched the *Sick Pilgrim* blog, and what started as a conversation between friends has spawned a group of writers from varied backgrounds and faiths, a podcast, a radio show, and a growing online community of hundreds who pray, question, and journey together in faith and doubt. Recently someone asked me (Jonathan), rather sarcastically, if Jess and I see *Sick Pilgrim* as our own little rebellion against the Catholic Church.

This person is a very respectable Catholic, married, two beautiful kids, active in her parish. This family would make the hall of fame for seemingly perfect Catholic families. I'm sure they would never present themselves that way, but I couldn't help but feel the pointed sarcasm in her question.

I guess she sees *Sick Pilgrim* as some kind of gallery of disreputable malcontents: the misfits, the angry, the agitators, the dissenters. I'm divorced, and I write about my struggles with my faith; I go to Mass in my lumberjack flannel shirts and bushy goatee. Jess jokes that she's a Catholic witch and writes openly about her occult attractions and her struggle with depression and personal brokenness.

But why would I want to rebel against the very thing I gave up everything—and I mean everything—to join three years ago? That would be insane.

We don't consider ourselves rebels. At least, we're not rebelling against the Catholic Church. The church is our only home, our family. It's where we have found our place. The growing *Sick Pilgrim* community includes priests, nuns, artists, writers, professors, theologians, the happily married, the divorced and widowed, single moms, single dads, the grief-stricken, persons who identify as LGBTQIA, farmer's moms, and everyone in between. There's no real template for what a sick pilgrim looks like—other than one of the heart.

True, it's usually a heart with a lot of open wounds or scar tissue. But none of us wants to remain in that wounded state. We are bound together on this journey by a deep, desperate desire to be healed, and the conviction (or suspicion) that this healing will come only through Jesus, present in the Eucharist, and in one another. So we lock arms and seek him together, throughout the strange landscapes of our strange lives.

If *Sick Pilgrim* wants to be anything at all, it's not a rebellion but a renewal, and we do pray, daily, that God will use us within the church. He's done this before, raised up ragtag groups of people and movements to remind his church of what he considers important. The apostles are the most obvious example. Other movements transformed the church for centuries, such as the monastic movement that rebelled against an empire, or St. Francis calling the medieval church back to its better self. There were Dorothy Day and the Berrigan brothers. And there are so many others, lesser known but deeply influential—such as our patron "saints," Frank Sheed and Maisie Ward, and their writer, Caryll Houselander, who had her own secret group, called "The Loaves and the Fishes."

Do we think *Sick Pilgrim* is any of the above? Our self-regard is not quite that high. But we do hope something good is coming out of what we do. And, that good, we hope, is that the misfits and outcasts and the people on the margins will begin to feel more at home in the Catholic Church, which truly is their home. As we've become so fond of saying, it's "*our* church too."

We don't want our own church. And we don't simply want a cool gang to hang with, though our community is a lot of fun. We don't want our own apostolate. We just want to be able practice our distinct vocations and to encourage others to do so, whatever they may be, in the context of this two-thousand-year-old faith. We want people to realize that Catholics have always been straight up freaks—and that the ones who look normal and perfect are the outliers, not us.

There are plenty of self-styled Catholic rebels who buck the church at every turn. They take pride in their outsider status and want to remain there. None of them wants to come "further up and further in," not realizing the solution to their struggle is not less of the Catholic Church but more. They need to blow past the pharisees into the deep mysteries of the Sacred Heart. Many have legitimate wounds and problems with the church, but they end up shaking their own pharisaical fingers at those they dislike. Others are converts, still wrestling with the deep wounds that can accompany conversion. Not to mention the sort of convert who is still so powered by the jet fuel of first love, so in love with the church that they remain, for a while, as blind to its flaws as they would be to any new lover's. What we want to say to all these folks is that the Catholic Church they love—or hate—is, in fact, the rebellion, a rebellion against the rulers, principalities, and powers. It's meant to change the world. Jesus says this to St. Peter very plainly when he gives him his commission to lead his Church: The gates of hell will never overcome it.

The church will be the ultimate victor, whatever the spirit of the age.

In the meantime, Christ has only this ragtag band of servants to be his hands and feet and to pour out his love on others. That's us. The whole church, not just *Sick Pilgrim*. We're strange people with strange ways. And we ain't always pretty. We get it wrong—a lot. But we must continue to fight the good fight.

It is good and just to rebel against the spirits of the age, wherever they are found, and especially when they infiltrate God's church. These spirits are tricky things; they can hide as the most orthodox, the most correct, the most Catholic. But when they lack the mercy and love of Christ, their theology is wrong, and we have every right as Catholics to rebel against them. But we oppose them by being agents of mercy, as Christ calls us to do. We oppose them by living out our personal vocations—whether priestly, or artistic, or domestic—in faith and in loving community.

As our role model Caryll Houselander once wrote, "The present agony of the world is ours; if we are Christians, we are bound to enter into it, to accept responsibility for it, to share to the full the work of defending, healing, saving, through hard work, through true contrition, through deep humility, through service."

This, we think, is the work Christ has given all of us. We believe the heart of God is mercy and love, and that we're not required to get everything right in our doctrine or in our lives. That's what becoming saints is all about. It's a process, a path, a walk—a pilgrimage—and it will not end until our deaths.

Because that's what the church is, in simplest terms: a journey. And it is for the sick and the strange.

ABOUT THE AUTHORS

JESSICA MESMAN GRIFFITH is a widely published writer whose work has been noted in *Best American Essays*. Her memoir, *Love and Salt: A Spiritual Friendship in Letters*, co-authored with Amy Andrews, won the 2014 Christopher Award for "literature that affirms the highest values of the human spirit." She is co-founder and curator of the blog *Sick Pilgrim*, "a rest stop for people who have Catholic minds or hearts or aesthetics or attractions and need companions for the journey." Jessica is a cultural columnist for *U.S. Catholic magazine*. Her articles and essays have also appeared in *Elle*, *Image*, *America*, *Christianity Today*, *Notre Dame Magazine*, *Busted Halo*, and *Living Faith*. Jessica is the co-founder of Trying to Say God: Re-enchanting the Catholic Imagination, a literary festival at the University of Notre Dame. She has spoken about spiritual writing and literary nonfiction at colleges and universities, the Festival of Faith and Writing, the Associated Writing Program's annual conferences, and the Neiman Conference for Narrative Journalism at Harvard University. She has appeared as a guest on NPR's *Interfaith Voices*, CBC's *Tapestry*, and on various shows for Relevant Radio and Sirius/

XM The Catholic Channel. Jessica has an MFA in creative writing from the University of Pittsburgh and was one of ten scholars selected by Patricia Hampl to complete a post-graduate Fellowship in the Erasmus Institute for Spiritual Autobiography at the University of Notre Dame.

JONATHAN RYAN is an author, columnist, speaker, and co-founder of Sick Pilgrim Media. He and co-founder Jessica Mesman Griffith created the *Sick Pilgrim* blog as a way to explore the edges of faith, reason, and doubt. Along with the online community, they started the *Wonder Podcast*. The *Library Journal* called Ryan's debut paranormal thriller, *3 Gates of the Dead* (Open Road Media), "a real attraction for fans of *The Exorcist* and the darker fiction of C. S. Lewis and Charles Williams." Book two in the series, *Dark Bride* (Open Road Media), was released in April 2015. Ryan has written for *Christianity Today*, *U.S. Catholic*, *Notre Dame Magazine*, *Quantum Fairy Tales*, and *Huffington Post*. He speaks frequently on writing, faith, and religion. Jonathan lives and works in Indianapolis, Indiana, where he works at a local parish.